# THE LAST DISCOURSE AND PRAYER
## OF OUR LORD

# THE
# LAST DISCOURSE AND PRAYER OF OUR LORD

*A STUDY OF ST JOHN XIV.–XVII.*

BY

## HENRY BARCLAY SWETE, D.D.

REGIUS PROFESSOR OF DIVINITY IN THE UNIVERSITY OF CAMBRIDGE
HON. CANON OF ELY; HON. CHAPLAIN TO THE KING

*οὐδέποτε ἐλάλησεν οὕτως ἄνθρωπος.*
*Κύριε, δίδαξον ἡμᾶς προσεύχεσθαι.*

WIPF & STOCK · Eugene, Oregon

Wipf and Stock Publishers
199 W 8th Ave, Suite 3
Eugene, OR 97401

The Last Discourse and Prayer of Our Lord
A Study of St. John XIV-XVII
By Swete, Henry Barclay
Softcover ISBN-13: 979-8-3852-1465-5
Hardcover ISBN-13: 979-8-3852-1466-2
eBook ISBN-13: 979-8-3852-1467-9
Publication date 1/25/2024
Previously published by Macmillan and Co., Limited, 1914

This edition is a scanned facsimile of the original edition published in 1914.

TO THE MEMORY OF

E. H. W. S.
S. A. S.
F. S. B.

Αὐτός, ὦ Φαίδων, παρεγένου Σωκράτει ἐκείνῃ τῇ ἡμέρᾳ ᾗ τὸ φάρμακον ἔπιεν ἐν τῷ δεσμωτηρίῳ, ἢ ἄλλου του ἤκουσας; Φαιδ. Αὐτός, ὦ Ἐχέκρατες. Εχ. Τί οὖν δή ἐστιν ἄττα εἶπεν ὁ ἀνὴρ πρὸ τοῦ θανάτου; . . . ἡδέως γὰρ ἂν ἐγὼ ἀκούσαιμι.

PLATO, Phaed.

## FOREWORD

THIS little book makes no claim to the character of a formal commentary. Its purpose is to offer help to any who may wish to combine a devout study of our Lord's last discourse and prayer with some attempt to gain a better understanding of the thought that lies beneath the surface of His words. I hope that it may serve this end more especially in Holy Week, when the Church of England reads St John xiv.-xvii. at daily mattins and evensong. The present volume will thus range with two earlier books, *The Appearances of our Lord after the Passion* (1907), and *The Ascended Christ* (1910), which were designed for use at Eastertide and Ascensiontide respectively.

With this aim I have banished to footnotes all references to the Greek text and any other matters which might break the thread of the reader's meditations. For the same reason I have limited myself to one view of passages which have received more than one interpretation. Critical problems have been almost wholly passed over, not as being unimportant but as foreign to the intention of this book.

There is, however, a preliminary question on which something must be said at the outset. Anyone who attempts to comment, however simply, upon one of the Johannine discourses may reasonably be asked to state the relation which he considers them to bear to words actually spoken by our Lord.

It has been urged, rightly as I think, that the sayings of Christ, even as they are recorded in our earliest Gospel and in those parts of the other Synoptic Gospels which are derived from an earlier lost document, cannot be regarded as the *ipsissima verba* of our Lord, since they have come to us through a translation and from sources which originally were not documentary but oral. In the case of the fourth Gospel further allowance must be made for the greater length of time that elapsed between the utterance of the sayings and their crystallization in a written shape. Moreover, it is clear that the author of this Gospel has set before himself a purpose which enables him to deal more freely with the form of the Lord's teaching than the Synoptists would have dealt. His rôle is that of the interpreter rather than the compiler; he seeks to impart to his readers the impression made upon his own mind by the person and teaching of Jesus. His prologue shews what that impression was, and the discourses expand the idea of the prologue. It was inevitable that the discourses should, in the circumstances, be coloured by their passage through the mind of the Evangelist; and there are places where he seems to comment on the words of the Lord rather than to record them. But that the discourses as a whole are the work of the author of the Gospel is inconceivable. When the reader passes from the prologue to the discourses, a subtle change of manner makes itself felt; in the former the disciple speaks, in the latter we hear the voice of the Master. The often repeated argument that the Synoptic Christ could not have spoken as the Johannine Christ does, appears to rest upon the assumption that the greatest of religious teachers (to take no higher ground) was incapable of varying either the method or the substance of His teaching when different circumstances called for such modification.

I regard, then, the earlier discourses in St John as genuine utterances of our Lord, cast in the form which they took in the thought of the great artist who planned the "spiritual Gospel." But for the last discourse and prayer I am disposed to claim something more. It is not, I think, unreasonable to suppose that words spoken on the last night of the Lord's life, in the privacy of the Upper Room, or, when that was left, of some other retreat where He was alone with the Eleven, produced an impression which could not be effaced; that at the end of a long life one who was present found almost the very words still ringing in his ears. If this were so, that disciple would assuredly have placed on record here his recollections of the Master's very words. Repeated study of these chapters confirms my conviction that they approach as near to the words actually spoken by our Lord as the memory of one who heard them can bring us, through the medium of a translation from Aramaic into Greek. There is in them a severe simplicity, a divine dignity, a mystery of paradox in which the reader catches sight of unexplored depths of truth ; features which, if not absent from the earlier discourses, are present here far more conspicuously. I cannot escape from the feeling that a greater than the greatest of Evangelists is here. That the last discourse and prayer of Jesus Christ rest upon no historical foundation, but represent only what the Evangelist conceived that the Incarnate Word would have said on the last night to His faithful disciples and to His Father in heaven, is to me altogether incredible. It is my hope that such a view may appear no less incredible to those who follow with me sentence by sentence through the words which St John assigns to the hours that immediately preceded the Agony, the Arrest, the Trials, and the Cross.

# CONTENTS

|  |  | PAGE |
|---|---|---|
| INTRODUCTION | - - - - - - - - | xiii |
| THE LAST DISCOURSE | | |
| Part I. - | - - - - - - - - | 1 |
| Part II. | - - - - - - - - | 69 |
| THE LAST PRAYER | - - - - - - - | 157 |

# INTRODUCTION

THE Last Discourse follows the departure of Judas Iscariot from the guest-chamber, the great upper room where our Lord and the Twelve were assembled for the Last Supper. Judas went forth from the company of the Twelve because he was not of them. There was no longer any possibility of keeping up the appearance of discipleship. The Master had exposed his treachery, and bidden him go quickly and do the thing on which he was resolved. We see the traitor rise silently, open the door, and disappear into the darkness of the night.[1] And now, for the first time during many months, Jesus felt Himself free from the presence of one who was officially a member of the Apostolic college, and at heart a devil;[2] at length He could speak freely, as among friends. Moreover, the action of Judas was, as He well knew, the signal for the coming of the last crisis; and the time had come to prepare His true disciples for it.

His first words to the Eleven proclaim His relief, and at the same time His consciousness of the approaching end. *When therefore he was gone out, Jesus saith, Now is the Son of man glorified,*[3] *and God is glorified in him; and God will glorify him in himself, and will glorify him forthwith* (xiii. 31 f.). The errand on which Judas had gone was

---

[1] xiii. 30 ἦν δὲ νύξ.      [2] vi. 70 διάβολός ἐστιν.

[3] On ἐδοξάσθη see Abbott, *Johannine Grammar*, 2446. The glorification is "past in relation to the spiritual order, though it was yet future in its historical realization" (Westcott).

## INTRODUCTION

to prepare the Lord's way to the Cross, and the Cross would be the supreme act of His life of service and sacrifice,[1] which is the true glory of His humanity and ours. The treachery of Judas was, though the traitor knew it not, for the glory of the Incarnate, and therefore for the glory of God, who was glorified by the perfect obedience of His Son, and would in turn glorify His Son by the glorious resurrection and ascension, the reward of His sacrifice and the expression of the inner glory of His life. "Forthwith," in a few short weeks, "God will glorify Him in Himself,"[2] by placing Him on His own throne, and acknowledging the oneness with Himself of the ascended Christ.

But the speedy glorification of Jesus, seen from the disciples' point of view, would have another aspect; to them it would speak of loss and grief beyond words. The Lord realizes this, and at once turns to them. *Children,[3] yet a little while I am with you; ye shall seek me, and as I said to the Jews, 'Where I go, ye cannot come,' so also I say now to you* (xiii. 33). He speaks to the Eleven as a father to his sons.[4] They are soon to be left in the world alone, and the words He had said to the hostile Jews some time ago would be true also in their case; both His enemies and His friends would seek Him in vain when He had left the world. But the words spoken to the Jews[5] in solemn warning[6] were now spoken to the disciples in loving sympathy, to prepare them for the life of faith.[5] Even from them the visible presence

---

[1] Chrysostom's explanation is scarcely adequate: τὸ γὰρ ἐν θανάτῳ γενόμενον περιγενέσθαι θανάτου δόξα μεγάλη. The Lord was glorified by His sacrifice and not only by His victory.

[2] *i.e.* ἐν τῷ θεῷ.

[3] τεκνία occurs in the fourth Gospel here only; in xxi. 5 παιδία is used.
[4] Cf. xiv. 18.   [5] vii. 34, viii. 21.

[6] viii. 21 ἐν τῇ ἁμαρτίᾳ ὑμῶν ἀποθανεῖσθε: xii. 35 ἵνα μὴ σκοτία ὑμᾶς καταλάβῃ. As Theodore of Mopsuestia remarks, τοῖς μὲν 'Ιουδαίοις

## INTRODUCTION

must be withdrawn, but only that the spiritual presence might be bestowed; for them "ye cannot come" speaks only of a temporary restriction, as He will presently shew.

Meanwhile, before He leaves His children, He will give them a last command. *A new commandment I give you: that ye love one another—as I loved you, that ye also love one another* (xiii. 34).

The commandment to love one's neighbour as one's self is as old as the Pentateuch,[1] and one of the great commandments on which all the Law and the Prophets hang. But the commandment that the children of Jesus Christ love their brethren in Him with a love answering to that with which they were all loved by Him, was new, and could not have been given before. This "law of Christ,"[2] this "love of the brethren" as it soon began to be called,[3] rests on new sanctions, opens new fields of energy, and is inspired by new motives and a new example. The Lord foresaw that it would become the distinctive 'note' of His disciples: *herein shall all know that ye are my disciples, if ye have love towards one another* (xiii. 35). Even the heathen, so Tertullian[4] tells us, realized this feature of the Christian life, exclaiming, "See how they love one another!" The new commandment created a new virtue, a peculiarly Christian form of love—a charity narrower in its scope than universal philanthropy, but deeper and more intense.[5]

ἐπέθηκε Καὶ οὐχ εὑρήσετε. Believers who seek shall find: "quaeramus inveniendum" (Augustine).

[1] Lev. xix. 18.         [2] Gal. vi. 2 τὸν νόμον τοῦ χριστοῦ.

[3] φιλαδελφία occurs already in 1 Thess. iv. 9, Rom. xii. 10; cf. Milligan's note on 1 Thess. *l.c.*

[4] *Apol.* 39 "vide, inquiunt, ut invicem se diligant." See Harnack, *Expansion of Christianity*, i. 181 ff.

[5] Cf. 2 Pet. i. 7 ἐν δὲ τῇ εὐσεβείᾳ τὴν φιλαδελφίαν, ἐν δὲ τῇ φιλαδελφίᾳ τὴν ἀγάπην.

It may be that the discourse would have ended here but for a question raised by Peter, which revealed the urgent need of further guidance. *Simon Peter saith to him, Lord, where goest thou?*[1] *Jesus answered, Where I go, thou canst not follow me now; but thou shalt follow me afterwards. Peter saith to him: Lord, wherefore cannot I follow thee, even now? I will lay down my life for thee. Jesus answereth, Lay down thy life for me, wilt thou? Verily, verily, I say to thee, The cock shall not crow till thou shalt have denied me thrice* (36 ff.).

The Lord's "I go," and "Where I go ye cannot come" still filled Peter's thoughts; he had no room there for the new commandment; the question whither the Lord was going and why the disciple could not follow clamoured for an answer. Jesus, knowing what was in Simon's mind, explained that he should follow later on, though not now.[2] But the vehement Apostle was not satisfied. Why not follow at once? If the way led through death, he was ready to die for the Master. Was he indeed? the Lord replies; that very night[3] would shew how far he was from reaching his own standard; so far that he would lack the courage even to bear reproach and contempt for the Master's sake. The Lord might have added other reasons why Peter could not follow Him yet. Before he followed, he had need to pass through the discipline of life, and be made perfect by suffering. And there was work to be done which for the moment was more needful than the offering of his life. Peter's hour had not

---

[1] Cf. the *Domine quo vadis?* of early tradition; the versions of the story are collected in Hastings, *D.B.* iii. 774.

[2] Origen, *in Joann.* t. xxxii. 3 ἔτι γὰρ εἶχεν ὁ Πέτρος τὸ μὴ ἐπιτρέπον αὐτῷ ἀκολουθεῖν τῷ λόγῳ ἤδη ποτέ. Cf. t. xix. 14.

[3] The ἀλεκτοροφωνία was the third watch of the night, roughly corresponding to 2-4 a.m. See Mc. xiii. 35.

yet come, and till it came he could not go where the Master went.

But to Peter himself and to the hitherto silent Ten the Lord's words brought increasing disquietude. The Master was going, they knew not whither. One thing only was clear; they could not follow Him, at least for the present; He would leave them behind and, as it seemed, without a guide, without a friend. The moment was one of the deepest gloom, unbroken by a single ray of light. The Lord knows this, and hastens to relieve their despair; and so the Great Discourse begins.

Δεῖ μνημονεύειν τῶν λόγων
τοῦ κυρίου Ἰησοῦ.

## I.

THE Lord comes at once to the great subject of His discourse: the grief of the disciples at His departure, and the comfort He has to offer them. *Let not your heart be troubled; believe in God, believe also in me* (xiv. 1).

Jesus can speak of heart-trouble from His own recent experience. He had "troubled Himself" at the sight of the mourners who grieved for the loss of Lazarus;[1] not many days ago His soul had been troubled by the near approach of the end;[2] this very evening His spirit had been disturbed by the treachery of Judas.[3] He knew that the human spirit can be tossed by sudden storms of grief or fear, like a sea tossed by winds.[4] And He knew also the only remedy for such agitation. "Father," He had cried in His own trouble, "save me from

---

[1] xi. 33 ἐτάραξεν ἑαυτόν.   [2] xii. 27 ἡ ψυχή μου τετάρακται.

[3] xiii. 21 ἐταράχθη τῷ πνεύματι.

[4] ταράσσεσθαι is used of a wind-swept sea in Isa. xxiv. 14 ταραχθήσεται τὸ ὕδωρ τῆς θαλάσσης, li. 15 ὁ ταράσσων τὴν θάλασσαν. The heart is in these chapters the seat of the emotions: cf. xiv. 27, xvi. 6, 22.

this hour: Father, glorify thy name."[1] He bids His disciples follow His example, and in their distress "believe in God."[2] But in their case, with their consciousness of sin and distance from God, more was needed; and He adds, "believe also in me":[3] 'in me also place your trust: in me whom you have followed these three years, with whom you have been in closest intercourse, and whom you have never known to fail you; in me who am man as you are, and yet can claim from you the same confidence that I myself as man repose in God.'

These first words have restored to the hearts of the Eleven a measure of the Lord's own calm. He can now unfold to them something more of the meaning and consequences of His departure, the bare mention of which had caused their trouble. *In my Father's house are many abodes; had it not been so, I would have told you, for I am going to make ready a place for you* (xiv. 2). "I am going,"[4] He repeats, though He now uses a word which speaks of His departure as a journey rather than as a per-

[1] xii. 27 f.

[2] πιστεύετε may be indicative here, Vulg. "creditis"; 'you do believe in God.' But the imperative yields on the whole the better sense: cf. Mc. xi. 22 ἔχετε πίστιν θεοῦ, and see Abbott, *Gr.* 2236 ff.

[3] πιστεύειν εἰς denotes an absolute transference of trust from oneself to another (Westcott).

[4] πορεύομαι, used also in xiv. 3, 12, 28, xvi. 7, 28; cf. Acts I. 10 f., I Pet. iii. 19, 22. ὑπάγω (xiii. 33, 36, xiv. 4, 5, 28, xvi. 5, 10, 17) emphasizes the departure—I go away, back, or home; see Abbott, *Johannine Vocabulary*, 1652, *Grammar*, 2082.

manent withdrawal from the world. 'I go my way, but whither? and why? My destination is my Father's house; and my purpose is to prepare for your journey thither.'

The words recall to us the first saying of the Lord's childhood,[1] and the first saying of His ministry at Jerusalem.[2] The Temple at Jerusalem was His Father's House on earth, until the unbelief of the Jews left it desolate. Our Lord was now on His way to that true House of God, of which the man-made sanctuary was but a figure. He could not describe it to them, for "eye never saw nor ear heard, nor did ever enter the heart of man all that God prepared for those that love him."[3] But there was one feature of the earthly Temple which might help them to realize their place in the heavenly. The Father's earthly house was not merely a sanctuary with its surrounding courts for worshippers; attached to it were chambers, some for the storing of things necessary for Divine service, some for the convenience of the priests or of the Sanhedrin.[4] It is perhaps in reference to those chambers that the Lord speaks of the "many mansions" in

[1] Lc. ii. 49 ἐν τοῖς τοῦ πατρός μου, *i.e.* ἐν τῇ οἰκίᾳ τοῦ πατρός μου. See Field, *Notes on the Translation of the N.T.* p. 51 ff.

[2] Jo. ii. 16 τὸν οἶκον τοῦ πατρός μου.

[3] 1 Cor. ii. 9.

[4] See Edersheim, *The Temple*, p. 29 ff.; Hastings, *D.B.* iv. 714 f.; *Encyc. Bibl.* iv. 4946.

the house not made with hands. "Mansions" has come into our Authorized and Revised versions through Tyndale from the Vulgate and Old Latin, where the word bears its proper meaning, 'places where a traveller halts and rests upon his journey.'[1] Many such chambers, such resting places, were to be found in the world to which the Lord was going. Let not the disciples think of the heavenly temple as a sanctuary where none could dwell but the Divine Majesty, but rather as a vast palace which could give shelter and rest to as many as the Lord willed. In its chambers, in close proximity to the Presence-Chamber of God, many, when their time for the great journey has come, will find rest and refreshment. Perhaps there is also latent in the word the thought that the future life is for the blessed a progress in which they "go from strength to strength,"[2] as men in a long journey go from halting place to halting place, until the end is reached.

The resting places are many, and, it is implied, sufficient for all; 'had it not been so,' the Lord adds, 'I would have told you,[3] for to make them

---

[1] For this sense of μονή, cf. Pausanias, x. 41 τέτμηται δὲ διὰ τῶν μονῶν ἡ ὁδός: *mansio* is similarly used in the title of a treatise ascribed to Ambrose, *De xlii mansionibus* (halting-places) *filiorum Israel*. μονή occurs again in this chapter (*v.* 23, *q.v.*).

[2] Ps. lxxxiv. 7.

[3] ὅτι πορεύομαι justifies ἂν εἶπον—'if there were no μοναί, or few, I could not have withheld from you this fact, for it would have changed my whole design.'

ready for you is the purpose of my journey.' As His own way had been prepared,[1] so the way of His disciples must be made ready by His entrance into the heavenly world. He is Himself the Forerunner[2] of the universal Church: the Church cannot enter until He has entered first; the mansions of His Father's house, though many, will stand empty, or without human occupants, unless He goes before to prepare a place for them.

Augustine[3] asks how this can be if, as we read in another Gospel, the Kingdom is prepared for us from the beginning of the world. The two views are, as he points out, complementary to each other; our place in the Father's house has been prepared in ages past by Divine predestination, and is now being prepared by the work of the Son. The latter preparation is conducted in the hearts and lives of men, but it depends on our Lord's life in heaven. The Lord's promise may be turned into the prayer, "Lord, prepare what Thou preparest, for Thou preparest us for Thyself."[4]

For all this we must trust Christ's word. Had

[1] ἑτοιμάζειν, the verb used here, occurs also in the classical passage Isa. xl. 3, which is cited in the N.T. as fulfilled in John the Baptist.

[2] Heb. vi. 20 πρόδρομος ὑπὲρ ἡμῶν εἰσῆλθεν Ἰησοῦς. See *The Ascended Christ*, c. vii.

[3] *tract. in Joann.* lxviii. 1: "et praeparavit et praeparat . . . praeparavit praedestinando, praeparat operando."

[4] *Ibid.* 3: "Domine, para quod paras, nos enim tibi paras."

there been no place for His disciples in His Father's house, no fellowship with Himself hereafter, no life hidden with Christ in God, He would have told them. He would not have suffered them to forsake all for His sake if He had had no bright hope to offer, no rest in store for them at their journey's end.

But there is more than this. His purpose to go and prepare for them assures them that He will return. *And if I should[1] go and make ready a place for you, I come again, and I will take you to be with myself* (xiv. 3). What would it avail to prepare the place if He did not come back, and Himself fetch them to fill it? How else would they find their way thither? Or how, if the way could be found, would they venture into the heavenly sanctuary, the very house and dwelling-place of God? A return, then, was involved in the very object of His journey: "if I go and prepare, I come again." The present tense "I come" is used rather than the future, for the Return is regarded not as a distant event, but as one ever imminent and at hand. The Lord says not, I will come, but "I come"; and so He speaks always both in the fourth Gospel[2] and in the Apocalypse:[3] the future is used only in Acts, where

[1] See Abbott, *Gr.* 2514. ἐάν, not ὅταν, is used, as in 1 Jo. iii. 2 ἐὰν φανερωθῇ: in neither passage is there any suggestion of a doubt, but the note of time which ὅταν would have struck has been avoided, apparently because it is foreign to the context.

[2] xiv. 18, 28, xxi. 22.

[3] Apoc. ii. 5, 16, iii. 11, xvi. 15, xxii. 7, 12, 20.

angels say "He shall come."[1] To Jesus Himself the Return is ever present; it is continually realizing itself in many ways; at any moment it may be realized by the world;[2] meanwhile He would have the Church think of it in terms of the present rather than of the future. Further, He would have His disciples connect His coming with the fulfilment of the purpose which He went to accomplish. He comes to take to Himself[3] those for whom He has prepared a place. As He had taken three of their number with Him to the Mount of the Transfiguration;[4] as that very night He would take the same three with Him to the Garden of the Agony;[5] so at His return He will take with Him not these three only but all the Eleven,[6] all the faithful, to the Father's House, to the many mansions prepared for them, that they may be with Him there, to see the glory which is the fruit of the Agony, and to see it not for a short hour, but for ever. The Father's House is the home of the Son, and those who are there are with the Incarnate Son, as He is with the Father.[7] This

[1] Acts i. 11 οὗτος ἐλεύσεται ὃν τρόπον ἐθεάσασθε αὐτὸν πορευόμενον.

[2] Apoc. I. 7 ἔρχεται ... καὶ ὄψεται αὐτὸν πᾶς ὀφθαλμός.

[3] παραλήμψομαι ὑμᾶς πρὸς ἐμαυτόν.

[4] Mc. ix. 2 παραλαμβάνει ... καὶ μετεμορφώθη ἔμπροσθεν αὐτῶν.

[5] Mc. xiv. 33 παραλαμβάνει ... μετ' αὐτοῦ.

[6] Cf. Euth. Zig. *ad loc.* ἱκαναὶ δέξασθαι καὶ ὑμᾶς.

[7] With πρὸς ἐμαυτόν cf. Jo. i. 1 ἦν πρὸς τὸν θεόν, and St Paul's phrase ἐνδημῆσαι πρὸς τὸν κύριον (2 Cor. v. 8). The force of πρός in this connexion is well illustrated by its use in Mt. xxvi. 18 (πρὸς σέ), Acts xi. 3.

is indeed the end for which the mansions have been made ready, as the next words shew: *that where I am, ye also may be* (xiv. 3*b*). The realized presence of Christ, and immediate communion with Him is the promise of the Return; it will restore, under new and permanent conditions, the direct intercourse of the Lord with His disciples which His departure interrupted. So little cause is there for hearts that love and trust Him to be disquieted by His withdrawal from them for a time. The purpose of the separation is to arrange an endless reunion.

## II.

FROM the purpose of the journey the Lord passes to the way. *And where I go, ye know the way* (xiv. 4). He does not say, as an inferior text makes Him say, "Ye know where I go."[1] Even now, after all that He had said, the Eleven did not grasp His destination. Where and what was the Father's House? The words suggested a temple fairer and greater than Herod's building, the archetype of the earthly fabric, a house not made with hands, eternal in the heavens; but how should mortal men, who had not ascended into heaven,[2] know what it was or where, or what it held in store? But the way they knew,[3] or at least the direction which it took, for they had seen the Master following it day by day. They knew whither His face ever turned, whither the steps of His most holy life carried Him. His whole life had been a journey to His Father's House; there remained now

---

[1] ὅπου ἐγὼ ὑπάγω οἴδατε, καὶ τὴν ὁδὸν οἴδατε (Vulg. "et quo ego vado scitis, et viam scitis"). The shorter reading is found in ℵBC*L.

[2] Cf. iii. 12 f.

[3] οἶδα is used throughout this passage, not γινώσκω. The disciples knew the facts, but did not recognize their true meaning.

only the last stage to complete it. Living with Him in daily closest fellowship they could not but know the way so far as it lay through the world; only the end and that which lay beyond it were hidden from their eyes.

Yet to the Eleven the saying was a hard one, and they could not hear it.[1] It did not illuminate; it even added to their perplexity. Their loyalty and trust were strained to the utmost by an appeal such as this, to which their consciousness made no response, against which their reason rebelled. Know the way? how could they when they did not know whither it led? One of them could no longer hold his peace. *Thomas saith to him, Lord, we know not where thou goest; how know we the way?* (xiv. 5). The destination must be determined, before the road that leads to it can be even approximately ascertained.[2]

If we had only the Synoptic Gospels, St Thomas would be to us little more than a name; the fourth Gospel lifts him out of obscurity by recording three sayings which reveal his character. It was Thomas who foresaw that the Master would meet His death at Jerusalem, and proposed to his fellow-disciples to "go and die with Him."[3] It was Thomas who refused any evidence of the Resurrection short of that of

---

[1] vi. 60.

[2] Euth. Zig. ᾤετο γὰρ αἰσθητὸν εἶναι τὸν τόπον . . . καὶ ὁδὸν ὁμοίως τοιαύτην.

[3] xi. 16 ἄγωμεν καὶ ἡμεῖς ἵνα ἀποθάνωμεν μετ' αὐτοῦ.

his own senses.[1] It was Thomas who now ventured to break into the Lord's discourse with a question which carried intellectual eagerness to the verge of unbelief. This blend of sincere devotion with the agnostic spirit is a paradox to which our own age supplies many parallels. For such enquirers, as for Thomas, the Lord has an answer, but not one which will immediately solve their difficulties.

*Jesus saith to him, I am the Way, and the Truth, and the Life ; none cometh to the Father except through me* (xiv. 6). 'You know the Way, since you know Me. I that speak, I who have been with you these three years, who am with you here and now, am myself the Way to the Father, and the only Way.'[2]

The conception is not easy; simple as are the words, the sense eludes the comprehension of a reader who contents himself with their surface meaning. We can think with less effort of our Lord as the Guide or the Example of life.[3] The Way is more; it is that without which Guide and Example would avail little, the primary condition of approach.

[1] xx. 25. See *Appearances of our Lord after the Passion*, ch. v.

[2] Thomas à Kempis (cited by Westcott): "sine via non itur; ego sum via." The Lord's saying reaches further; He says plainly: "sine h a c via ad Patrem non itur."

[3] Hort, *The Way, the Truth, and the Life*, p. 20: "These phrases may exact a slighter effort of thought, but only because they belong at best to a rudimentary and transitory form of truth."

A "way of God" is not unknown to the Old Testament. "The meek," says the Psalmist, "will he teach his way";[1] "teach me thy way," he or another psalmist prays.[2] The Way of God is the "way of righteousness," the "way of life"; the opposite of man's own way, which is that "of death."[3] All this was familiar to Israel before the Incarnation. But no prophet, no righteous man in Israel had dared to say, 'I am the way; in me all God's purpose is revealed, and all His will is fulfilled. Not only have I in all things followed the Way of God; I am myself that Way; in me it finds perfect expression, and in me alone.'

But there is more than this in our Lord's claim to be the Way. The Way of God is also in Him the Way to God.[4] Across the infinite gulf which parts the human from the Divine, the creature from the Creator, the sinner from the Holy One, Jesus has thrown a permanent Way in His own Incarnate Life and Death. By that Way He Himself passed into the Presence of God; by the same will pass all who come to God through Him. He goes to the Father in right of His Sonship, His sinless obedience, His fulfilment of all righteousness; His disciples go in

[1] Ps. xxv. 9.      [2] Ps. lxxxvi. 11.

[3] Isa. xxxv. 8, Jer. xxxi. 3. Cf. the opening words of the *Didache*: ὁδοὶ δύο εἰσί, μία τῆς ζωῆς καὶ μία τοῦ θανάτου.

[4] Cf. xiii. 3 πρὸς τὸν θεὸν ὑπάγει.

virtue of their union with Him; He is their Way, as He was His own.

"I am the Truth," the Lord adds, "and the Life"; two new conceptions which seem to break the sequence of the thought, for the next words, "No man cometh to the Father except through me," arise directly out of "I am the Way." But "the Truth" and "the Life" are in fact but other aspects of "the Way," bringing out its meaning more clearly, and so preparing for that which follows, as we shall presently see.

Truth is one of St John's characteristic words,[1] and it is more than once associated by this Gospel with our Lord. "The Word ... dwelt among us ... full of grace and truth." "If ye abide in my word ... ye shall know the truth, and the truth shall set you free." "To this end have I been born and to this end I am come into the world, that I should bear witness unto the truth; every one that is of the truth heareth my voice." Pilate retorted, "What is truth?" little knowing that the Very Truth stood before him in the person of Jesus.[2]

Truth, as St John conceives it, is the opposite both of falsehood and of that which is shadowy and unsubstantial. Both find their negation in Christ.

---

[1] ἀλήθεια occurs in the fourth Gospel twenty-five times, as against seven in the Synoptic Gospels.

[2] i. 14, 17, viii. 31 f., xviii. 37 f.

He is the Truth itself which cannot lie;[1] His words, His actions, His very Self are absolute verity. He is also the Truth as opposed to the unrealities of life. The world is full of things that perish in the using; our way through it is strewn with unfulfilled promises and disappointed hopes. Even the Law had but a "shadow of good things to come"; in the Gospel only we have "the very image of the things."[2] The Gospel is "the word of truth,"[3] inasmuch as it reveals God in Christ; the Christian life, so far as it is true to its conception, is a 'walking in the truth';[4] it realizes the actualities of the spiritual world, and lays hold on eternal life, the only "life which is life indeed."[5] It does this, because it is life in Christ who is the Truth, or rather it is Christ, the Truth, living in us.

For Christ, as He is the Truth, so is He also the Life. Life is another Johannine word,[6] and closely connected with this Evangelist's doctrine of the person of Christ. "In him was life." "As the Father hath life in himself, even so gave he to the Son to have life in himself." The life of the Word was communicated to the Creation, and more especially

---

[1] As the Very Image of the ἀψευδὴς θεός (Tit. i. 2).

[2] Heb. x. 1, cf. Jo. i. 17.   [3] Eph. i. 23, Col. i. 5.   [4] 2 Jo. 4.

[5] 1 Tim. vi. 19 τῆς ὄντως ζωῆς. Cf. Ignatius, *Trall.* 9 οὗ χωρὶς τὸ ἀληθινὸν ζῆν οὐκ ἔχομεν.

[6] ζωή occurs in the fourth Gospel thirty-seven times.

to man, who partakes of the rational nature of the Creator; "the life was the light of man."[1] The Incarnation of the Word brought fresh and fuller supplies of the Divine life to a humanity to which sin had brought death. "I came that they may have life, and have it more abundantly." "I am the Resurrection and the life."[2] The new life, which is the fruit of the Incarnation, comes through seeing the Son and believing on Him; through eating His flesh and drinking His blood. His very words are spirit and life; they are the words of eternal life; His person is this life itself.[3]

Let us try to correlate the three titles which our Lord claims. "I am the Way and the Truth and the Life." In the Latin versions a happy alliteration suggests the close connexion which exists between the three: "Ego sum Via et Veritas et Vita." He is the Way which leads through the Truth to the Life. Or, reversing the order, as we may, He is the Life which is the Truth, and being the Life and the Truth He is also the Way. The three cannot be separated in our experience. As we live the life, we know the truth, and advance on the way; as we follow the way, we learn the truth and are filled with the life.

He who is the Life and the Truth is also the Way to the Father. To bring us to God was the purpose

[1] i. 4. Cf. Athan, *de incarn.* 3.   [2] x. 10, xi. 25.   [3] vi. 40, 54, 63, 68.

of the Incarnation, the Passion, the Resurrection and Ascension;[1] through the incarnate, crucified, risen, ascended Christ "we have our access."[2] Through the veil of the incarnate life "a new and living way" leads us to the Divine Presence. The way is open to all, and there is no other. For our Lord's great offer has a negative side which must not be overlooked. It comes into sight frequently in this Gospel: "Except a man be born from above he cannot enter"; "no man can come to me except the Father which sent me draw him"; "except ye eat and drink ... ye have not life in yourselves."[3] And now: "none cometh to the Father except through me." From one point of view the Gospel is exclusive; its very comprehensiveness, its Divine sufficiency, forbids an alternative. It is another question how inclusive the One Way may be. Many, it may be, have travelled over it and reached the end with little knowledge of Christ or none; saints of generations before He came, saints who never heard His name, and yet in some measure partook of the truth and the life. It is enough to know that all who have reached the Father's house have come through Him,[4] and that all who come through Him attain at last.

---

[1] 1 Pet. iii. 18 ἵνα ὑμᾶς προσαγάγῃ τῷ θεῷ.

[2] Eph. ii. 18 δι' αὐτοῦ ἔχομεν τὴν προσαγωγήν.   [3] iii. 5, vi. 44, 53.

[4] In δι' ἐμοῦ the preposition refers to the Way, but to the Way as a personal agent. A suggested reference to our Lord as the Door (Jo. x. 9) seems improbable and unnecessary.

## III.

*If ye had come to know me, ye would have known*[1] *my Father also. From henceforth ye are learning to know him, and have seen him* (xiv. 7).

'Your perplexities about my journey, as to the way and the end, would not have arisen if you had used your opportunities of coming to know who and what I am. For then you would have known what my Father is, as a face becomes familiar through the study of a faithful portrait; your acquaintance with the Son would have entailed some knowledge of Him whose Son I am. But the time is coming, and indeed has now come, when the Father Himself shall be revealed to you: what you failed to learn from your intercourse with me during the years of the Ministry, you will gain through my death, resurrection, ascension; the eyes of your understanding will shortly be opened by the Spirit to see the King in His beauty; to behold the Father in His Son.'

[1] εἰ ἐγνώκειτε . . . ἂν ᾔδειτε. Or, to borrow a phrase from Job xxii. 21 (A.V., R.V.): "If ye had acquainted yourselves with me," etc. For ἂν ᾔδειτε ℵD* read γνώσεσθε, and AD² ἐγνώκειτε ἄν—both apparently corrections. In viii. 19 ᾔδειτε is used twice.

Strange that the revelation of the Father should come to the Eleven not through the visible presence of the Word made flesh, not through His works or words, but through a presence removed from sight, spiritualized, taken back into the Father's House, out of the sight of the eye and the hearing of the ear! "We beheld His glory, glory as of the only begotten from the Father."[1] So writes St John in his prologue, looking back on the days of the flesh as they were seen afterwards in the light of the Spirit; but at the time neither St John nor any other could see far beneath the surface of the great life in the presence of which they spent their days. The Only-begotten who was in the Father's bosom declared Him to them by every act and word, and yet they knew Him not. Now at last when Jesus was leaving them, the light was beginning to dawn upon them; henceforth they would know God with a knowledge derived from fellowship, from seeing Him who is invisible and living in His sight, through their access to Him by the new and living Way, through the Son and in the Spirit of the Son which they should presently receive.

At this point another of the Eleven, emboldened by the example of Thomas, breaks in with a remark. *Philip saith to him, Lord, shew us the Father, and it is enough for us* (xiv. 8). Of Philip as of Thomas

---

[1] i. 14.

our knowledge comes chiefly from St John. He was of Bethsaida, the fishing town on the sea which also gave to the Apostolate St Andrew and St Peter. The Lord had found and called Philip after His return to Galilee from the Baptism. It was Philip who had answered Nathanael's doubt by "Come and see"; whom the Lord had proved by the question, "Where are we to buy bread that these may eat?" to whom Greeks, perhaps attracted by his Greek name, came with the petition, "Sir, we would see Jesus," and who, with Andrew, "told Jesus" of their desire.[1] And now it is Philip who, when he hears that he and his fellow-disciples henceforth know the Father, and have even seen Him, cannot repress the cry, "Lord, shew us the Father, and we ask nothing more." Perhaps he remembered how under the Old Covenant the seventy elders of Israel "saw the God of Israel";[2] and how Moses made bold to ask, "Shew me now thy ways"—"shew me thy glory," and the Lord in answer to that prayer had made His glory pass by and proclaimed His name.[3] Had not Jesus, whom they knew to be greater than Moses, received such a revelation for them? They asked nothing better, for what better or greater thing could they wish for? But assuredly they had not seen this great sight, the

---

[1] i. 44, 46, vi. 5, xii. 21 f.  [2] Exod. xxiv. 10.
[3] Exod. xxxiii. 13, 18, xxxiv. 5 ff.

Father's glory, hitherto; and until they had seen it their greatest need was unsupplied.

The Lord's answer was unexpected and disappointing. *Jesus saith to him, Am I so long a time with you, and thou hast not come to know me, Philip?*[1] *He who hath seen me hath seen the Father; how sayest thou, Shew us the Father?* (xiv. 9). All those months in Galilee they had seen the God of Israel in the face of Jesus Christ; they had lived with the Father's very image, and had not known it. God had passed by and proclaimed His name to them, not in a transient vision, as to Moses, but in the human form and speech and life of the Only begotten.[2] And yet Philip, who was herein the spokesman of the rest, looked for a greater manifestation: a revelation of the Father distinct from His revelation of Himself in the Son. Nothing less would content them; their long intercourse with the Incarnate Word left them still hankering after a display of the Divine glory greater than that which for so long a time they had daily seen. What was this but a confession that they had never known the Master whom they followed? To see Him was to see the Image of the invisible God, and yet they who had seen Him asked that they might be

---

[1] As Westcott points out, "there is an evident pathos in this direct personal appeal." The position of Φίλιππε at the end of the sentence rather than after εἰμί intensifies the appeal.

[2] Cf. i. 18 θεὸν οὐδεὶς ἑώρακεν πώποτε· μονογενὴς θεὸς . . . ἐκεῖνος ἐξηγήσατο. Col. i. 15 ὅς ἐστιν εἰκὼν τοῦ θεοῦ τοῦ ἀοράτου.

shewn the Father in some other and more glorious form. Such a demand betrayed either ignorance or incredible unbelief.

*Believest thou not that I am in the Father and the Father is*[1] *in me? The words that I say to you I speak not from myself, but the Father abiding in me doeth his works. Believe me that I am in the Father, and the Father in me; or if not, believe me because of the works themselves* (xiv. 10 f.).

Our Lord's appeals to faith vary in proportion to the opportunities of those who are addressed. The man who was born blind and received his sight is asked, "Dost thou believe in the Son of Man?" To Martha, sister of dead Lazarus, He puts the question, "Believest thou this?" that is, that "I am the Resurrection and the Life." Philip, who had been long with Jesus, is put to a severer test, 'Believest thou not that I and my Father are one by mutual indwelling; that I am in Him, and He is in Me?' So in the history of the Church the creed grew, and faith became at once fuller and harder. The simple confession of the first days that "Jesus is Lord"[2] was expanded into the Roman creed of the second century, the Nicene creed of the fourth, the *Quicumque* of the fifth or sixth. The creed grows more complex as

[1] The position of ἐστιν at the end of the sentence marks emphasis—"the Father truly is in me" (Abbott, *Gr.* 2579).

[2] Rom. x. 9, 1 Cor. xii. 3, Phil. ii. 11.

the centuries advance. Our own age calls for a return to primitive simplicity in the *credenda* of the Church. Christ asks not for less faith, but for more, in proportion as our knowledge is greater; "to whomsoever much is given, of him shall much be required."

The mutual indwelling of the Father and the Son was not revealed for the first time in the Last Discourse; it had been taught early in the Ministry, and, according to St John, even to the Jews. "The Son," Jesus had said, "can do nothing of Himself but what He seeth the Father doing; for what things soever He doeth, these the Son also doeth in like manner." "My teaching is not mine, but His that sent me." "I and the Father are one ... the Father is in me, and I in the Father.[1] The Jews had frankly disbelieved these great claims; could it be that His own disciples doubted, or had they only failed to grasp things too great and high for their understanding? On the latter supposition the Lord now brings the mystical coinherence of the Father and the Son within their comprehension by stating it in the terms of their own experience. They remembered His words and His works, but these were the fruits of the Father's indwelling. The words of eternal life that He spoke, the works that none other man did, were not from Himself, but from the Father. A human

[1] v. 19, vii. 16, x. 30, 38.

will, human brains, human hands were at work, but behind them and with them the Divine wrought as the source and the motive power of all. The words of Christ were His own, and yet not from Himself; His works were His own, and yet they were the works of Him that sent Him, not merely inasmuch as He was sent to do them, but because of the abiding presence in Him of the Father. Thus He can speak of "the works which I do,"[1] and yet say, as He does here, that "the Father abiding in Him doeth His—the Father's—works."[2] " My Father worketh hitherto and I work "[3] does not describe two workers or two works, but the co-operation of two Persons in one substance. All the Father's works are also the Son's, and all the Son's are the Father's, seeing that the Two are one in essence and in operation. In the historical Jesus the Son was incarnate, and with the Incarnate Son there was the inseparable Presence and Energy of the Eternal Father.

What proof does the Lord offer of this mystery of Divine coinherence? In the first place, His own word; as secondary and collateral evidence, His works. "Believe me[4] that I am in the Father, and the Father in

[1] x. 25 τὰ ἔργα ἃ ἐγὼ ποιῶ.

[2] ὁ πατὴρ ποιεῖ τὰ ἔργα αὐτοῦ. So ℵBD; the reading αὐτὸς ποιεῖ τὰ ἔργα, Vulg. "ipse facit opera," rests on A and the later uncial MSS.

[3] v. 17 ὁ πατήρ μου ἕως ἄρτι ἐργάζετα, κἀγὼ ἐργάζομαι.

[4] πιστεύετε: cf. οὐ πιστεύεις; in v. 10. The Lord now turns from Philip to the Eleven as a body.

me; or if [ye believe me] not, believe because of the works themselves" (xiv. 11).[1] 'Take my word for the fact, or if you cannot trust me so far, let the Father's works, manifested in my life, convince you of its truth.' To men who had experienced for so long the absolute trustworthiness of the Speaker, who knew Him for the Truth itself, His mere word should have sufficed. To the believer no other proof should be necessary but his faith: he trusts Christ implicitly, and it is enough that Christ has said it. But the Lord condescends to the weakness of a faith which has not reached maturity, and for this imperfect faith there remained the guarantee of acts, not one or two, but innumerable, which were palpably Divine. To accept Jesus as the Son of God on the evidence of miracles was not worthy of men who had been the daily companions of His most holy life, but it was better than not to believe in Him at all. There is pathos in the alternative which Jesus offers to the Eleven, "If ye believe me not, believe because of the works."[2] The works of Christ were not designed to serve as a basis for faith, but they might fulfil that purpose so long as the disciples needed any other assurance than the Master's word.

In our time the miracles are so far from assisting faith that they are a stumbling-block to many, while

[1] Even Nicodemus had gone as far as this (Jo. iii. 2).
[2] Cf. x. 38 (to the Jews) κἂν ἐμοὶ μὴ πιστεύητε, τοῖς ἔργοις πιστεύετε.

others save their faith by sacrificing the historical truth of these works of Christ. Our Lord, as St John represents Him, assumes the truth of the miracles, but allows them only a secondary place as witnessing to His oneness with the Father. Their witness is not necessary to those who have learnt to trust Christ Himself.

## IV.

*Verily, verily I say to you, He that believeth in me, the works that I do, he also shall do; yea and greater than these shall he do, because I am going to the Father* (xiv. 12).

'The faith of which I speak—so the Lord seems to say—whether it is based on my works or (which is better) on my words, finds its object in myself; and faith in me sets up such unity of purpose and action between me and the believer that he will do that which I do; nay more, since my journey to the Father will bring fresh power and energy, he will do even more than I did when I was in the flesh.'

Even during the Ministry the Twelve received power to do as their Master did. "He gave them authority over unclean spirits, and they cast out many devils, and anointed with oil many that were sick and healed them."[1] So we read in St Mark, and St Matthew adds, perhaps from an earlier record of our Lord's sayings, that He bade them "raise the dead, cleanse the leper."[2] Such works of physical heal-

[1] Mc. vi. 7, 13.     [2] Mt. x. 8.

ing continued to be wrought in the Church, not only during the lifetime of the Apostles, but if we may trust Justin, Irenaeus, and other early Christian witnesses,[1] in the second and third centuries, although with decreasing frequency. As late as the fifth century a writer, who is by no means disposed to be credulous,[2] admits that "some things are still done in answer to prayer," and expresses the belief that if these are miracles, miracles will never cease in the Church till the Lord returns. Whatever may be thought of this doctrine, it will be observed that the Lord Himself extends to all believers the power to do as He does, making faith the only condition of Christlike work.[3] The works of Christ, however, were not all miraculous; even more characteristic than the miracles were the acts of self-sacrifice and submission to the Divine will, which abounded in His earthly life. And these in a measure are reproduced in all believers. Far more difficult are the words that follow; "Yea, and greater works than these shall he (that is, the believer) do." Of "greater works" the reader of St John has heard already: "yea, and greater works than these shall He (the Father) shew Him (the

---

[1] Justin, *Apol.* ii. 6; *Tryph.* 39; Irenaeus, ii. 31. 2, 32. 4; Tertullian, *Apol.* 37; Origen, *c. Cels.* I. 2, 46.

[2] Theodore of Mopsuestia on 2 Thess. ii. 6. So also his great contemporary in the West: "etiam nunc fiunt miracula in eius nomine, sive per sacramenta eius sive per orationes" (Aug. *civ. Dei*, xxii. 87).

[3] Cf. 1 Cor. xiii. 2 κἂν ἔχω πᾶσαν τὴν πίστιν ὥστε ὄρη μεθιστάνειν.

Son) that ye may wonder."[1] But these greater works are still the Son's, and the words say no more than that the wonder of the Ministry will grow as time goes on. Here we have a bewildering extension of the prophecy: the greater wonders are to come when the Ministry is past and the Lord is gone. The disciple is to do greater things than the Master, the believer to exceed the works of the Christ. Yet, to think of the miracles first, what could be greater than to raise the dead, to feed a multitude with the food of a handful of men, to still the sea at a word, to turn water into wine! Nor, as a matter of fact, has the history of the Church any greater miracles to shew than those attributed to the Lord in the four Gospels. But the works of Christ are not to be limited to the miracles,[2] nor were these in His own judgement the greatest. When He sent the disciples of the Baptist to their master with a record of the wonders they had seen and heard, the highest place in the ascensive scale is given not to the raising of the dead, but to the preaching of the Gospel to the poor.[3] If we follow this significant hint, it brings us at once to a fulfilment of Christ's promise that His disciples shall do greater things than He had done. There is

[1] v. 20.

[2] The Lord does not say μείζονα σημεῖα, but, as the context shews, μ. ἔργα—a more inclusive word.

[3] Mt. xi. 5 νεκροὶ ἐγείρονται, καὶ πτωχοὶ εὐαγγελίζονται. Luke has the same order (vii. 22).

nothing in the record of His ministry to be compared with the conversion and baptism of the three thousand on the great Day of Pentecost; nothing like the work of St Paul in spreading the Gospel and planting the Church in four great provinces of the Empire. Our Lord's ministry was nearly limited to the tetrarchy of Herod, and even within those narrow bounds, He had little success; the crowds which hung upon His lips melted away; the movement was evanescent, and even the little flock which clung to Him were men "of little faith," undiscerning, as these chapters shew, and, as it seemed, ill-prepared to carry on His work. Judged by outward appearances His ministry was a failure; certainly it achieved few immediate results. Greater things were done by the Eleven, by St Paul and his followers, by the Church of the early centuries; greater things are being done by the Church of the present age.

The Lord foresaw the remarkable extension of Christian activity which would follow His departure, and not only foresaw, but accounted for it. 'It must be so, for I[1] am going unto the Father.' This very journey which seems to put an end to all chance of success, is the condition of increased power and efficiency. 'My departure will add immeasurably to your resources, not because it takes

[1] "I" is emphatic, and so is "to the Father" (ἐγὼ πρὸς τὸν πατέρα πορεύομαι). It is not the journey which will have this effect, but the return of the Person who goes to the Person to whom He goes.

me from the world, but because it brings me to the Father. For I go to receive for you that which you could not have while I was with you. You shall do greater things than I have done, because you shall have larger powers granted to you through my presence in the Father's house.'

So the mystery is partly explained. It is not we who do greater things than Christ, but Christ, ascended and glorified, who does greater things than Christ in the days of His flesh. As Augustine says, both the works of the Ministry, of which we read in the Gospels, and the works which are done in the Church from the Pentecost to our own day are the works of Christ: the former were done by Him in person, the latter are done by His Spirit in believers.[1] All the great Christian exploits of the past nineteen centuries are *gesta Christi* no less truly than the Gospel miracles, and they are greater than the greatest of those miracles. Men can and often do hesitate to regard the miracles as historical; but the most unsparing criticism cannot refuse to admit the changes wrought in the world by the faith and Spirit of Christ. What is the raising of the widow's son or of Lazarus compared with the quickening of countless lives through the Sacraments and preaching of the Church?

[1] Aug. *tract. in Joann.* lxxi. 1: "ego facturus sum et tunc maiora quam nunc; maiora per eum qui credit in me quam praeter eum per me." Cf. lxxi. 3: "illud per se, hoc per ipsos; sed tamen utrumque ipse."

## ST JOHN xiv. 12–14

What is the turning of water into wine compared with the turning of moral weakness into strength, and of common things in daily use into the communion of the Body and Blood of Christ?

Greater works than those of a visible Christ shall the Church do in the power of His invisible presence. Yet these greater works are not to be done automatically, or without spiritual effort on the part of believers; they are to be done in answer to prayer. So the Lord continues: *And whatsoever ye shall ask in my name, this will I do, that the Father may be glorified in the Son. If ye shall ask* [me][1] *anything in my name, this will I do* (xiv. 13 f.).

The Sermon on the Mount had taught the general lesson that he who would receive anything from God must ask for it.[2] The Last Discourse adds that the believer in Christ must ask in Christ's name. The exact phrase meets us here for the first time, but once uttered, it is frequently repeated in the Discourse.[3] Its meaning may be gathered from the Lord's use elsewhere of the words "in my Father's name." When He says "I have come in my Father's name ... another shall come in his own name"[4] He clearly means, 'I represent my Father's mind and will; others will represent none but their own.' When He speaks of "the works that I do in my

---

[1] $+\mu\epsilon$ ℵB (om. ADL).  
[2] Mt. vii. 7 f.; cf. Lc. xi. 9 f.  
[3] xiv. 26, xv. 16, xvi. 23 f., 26.  
[4] v. 43.

Father's name,"[1] He regards Himself as acting by His Father's authority and power. According to the analogy of these and other passages, to ask in Christ's name is to ask as on behalf of Christ, as belonging to Him, and authorized by Him to approach the Father. It is not the use of the formula *through Jesus Christ* that gains acceptance for our prayer, as though it possessed a magic power to unlock the treasuries of Divine mercy and grace. The formula serves its purpose if it reminds us that we approach God in our prayers not as having in ourselves any claim to be heard, but as identified with His Son our Lord, with whom He is "well pleased,"[2] whom the Father hears and answers always.[3]

Twice over the Lord assures us that He will do whatsoever we thus ask.[4] "I will do it," that is 'I will make it my business to see that the thing is done.'[5] Christian prayer is normally addressed to the Father, but the answer comes through the Son. It belongs to the glorified Christ to carry into effect the Father's will, to bestow the Father's gifts, in virtue of the universal authority committed to Him in heaven and on earth. In fulfilling this office He not only consults our interest, but He acts for the greater glory of God: His purpose is "that the

---

[1] x. 25.     [2] Mt. iii. 17, xvii. 5     [3] xi. 42.

[4] xiv. 13, 14 τοῦτο ποιήσω: the emphatic pronoun is used the second time.

[5] So Apollinarius: ἴδιον δὲ αὐτοῦ τὸ ἔργον ἐνδείκνυται.

## ST JOHN xiv. 13, 14

Father may be glorified in the Son." Of His life on earth He could say, "I seek not mine own glory,"[1] and the words are true also of His heavenly life. The aim of His present sovereignty as of His earthly service is the glory of the Father, which reveals itself in the work of Him who is the very image of His Father's substance. In every answer to his prayer the believer sees afresh the glory of God reflected in "the might of Jesus Christ our Lord."

Augustine[2] asks how Christ's "whatsoever" is to be reconciled with the facts of Christian experience, which shews that many things asked for by the faithful are withheld for their own good. His answer is that "whatsoever" is limited by "in my name," which excludes prayers that are not in agreement with our Lord's saving purpose, or with the Divine foreknowledge and will.

[1] viii. 50.

[2] *tract. in Joann.* lxxiii. 2. He adds that even petitions which are according to God's will are not always granted at the time; but in such cases "differtur quod petimus, non negatur."

## V.

HITHERTO the Lord has urged upon His disciples the duty of faith in Him;[1] now He adds His claim upon their love, or rather, presupposing that they love Him, points out that the proof of love is obedience. *If ye love me, ye will keep my commandments* (xiv. 15). He has no doubt of their love; when Judas left the supper-room, the only disloyal member of the company vanished. Nor, if they loved Him sincerely, was there need to insist on obedience to His express directions. Therefore He does not say "Keep," but "Ye will keep";[2] the observance of His injunctions will follow as a necessary consequence. The Eleven would carry them out, because they were His: literally and without intelligence, it might be, without appreciation of their purpose or necessity, out of mere devotion to His person. To this point the Lord will presently return;[3] for the moment He is content to strike the note, for another subject calls for attention first. He has a promise to make, the greatest that can be

[1] xiv. 1, 10 ff.     [2] τηρήσετε (ℵ)BL, τηρήσατε AD Latt.
[3] See verses 21, 23.

made: a promise which is at once the reward of obedient love, and the best guarantee of guidance and inspiration to those who love and obey to the extent of their present power. *And I will ask the Father, and he will give you another Advocate to be with you while the world lasts,*[1] *the Spirit of truth* (xiv. 16, 17 a). That is to say, 'When I have reached the Father's house and am in direct communication with Him, I will seek from Him this gift.' Of the two verbs which are translated 'ask,'[2] St John uses here the one which implies free intercourse and exchange of thought, as between those who meet face to face, rather than the relation of a suppliant to his superior.[3] It is enough for the Son to make known His desire: " Father, I will "[4] suffices, for His will and the Father's are one. And this is so even in reference to the greatest request that He can make: " I will ask . . . and He shall give you another Paraclete."

[1] Cf. εἰς τὸν αἰῶνα in Mc. xi. 14, Lc. i. 55, Jo. xiii. 8, 1 Cor. viii. 13. The phrase may have a far wider outlook (Jo. vi. 51, 58, x. 28, xi. 26, 2 Jo. 2, etc.), but in the present context it seems better to interpret it as = εἰς τὴν συντέλειαν τοῦ αἰῶνος τούτου.

[2] αἰτεῖν or αἰτεῖσθαι (xiv. 13 f., xv. 7, 16, xvi. 23 f., 26), and ἐρωτᾶν (xiv. 16, xvi. 5, 19, 23, 26, 30, xvii. 9, 15, 20).

[3] St John invariably uses ἐρωτᾶν in reference to the Son's approaches to the Father. But the distinction between ἐρωτᾶν and αἰτεῖν had, as the papyri shew, broken down before the first century, and in the Epistles ἐρωτᾶν is used freely of making requests (Phil. iv. 3, 1 Thess. iv. 1, v. 12, 2 Thess. ii. 1, 1 Jo. v. 16, 2 Jo. 5). Still ἐρωτᾶν does not represent the petitioner as a suppliant, and is therefore more appropriate to our Lord than αἰτεῖν or αἰτεῖσθαι.

[4] Jo. xvii. 24.

The word "Paraclete" has a considerable history.[1] In the Greek law courts it denoted 'a friend at court,' the unpaid advocate who pleaded the defendant's[2] cause. Philo used it to describe his Logos, regarded as the High Priest of men, who pleads for them with God.[3] So St John speaks in his first epistle of the glorified Christ as our Paraclete with the Father.[4] The word passed into Aramaic,[5] and its use in the Gospel seems to suggest that it had been applied to Jesus or adopted by Him to express His own relation to the Twelve. He had been, while He lived, their powerful friend, counselling and protecting them, ready when they were attacked to take their part, maintaining their cause against all comers. He was going to the Father to be the Advocate of all believers in the court of heaven, but at the cost of His visible presence being withdrawn from the Church on earth. Hence the need of another Advocate,[6] who should never depart so long as the world lasted.

---

[1] A full discussion of the word παράκλητος will be found in Westcott's Additional Note on c. xiv. 16, 26, and in Lightfoot, *On a Fresh Revision of the English N.T.* p. 50ff.; or see Hastings, *D.B.* iii. p. 665ff. *s.v.*

[2] Cf. Demosth. *de falsa leg.* 341.

[3] Philo, *de vit. Moys.* iii. 24.

[4] 1 Jo. ii. 1 παράκλητον ἔχομεν πρὸς τὸν πατέρα, Ἰησοῦν Χριστὸν δίκαιον.

[5] פְּרַקְלִיט (Pirqe Aboth, iv. 15), פְּרַקְלִיטָא.

[6] The rendering "Comforter" in the Gospel comes to us from Wycliffe, and has been retained by the later English versions including the text of the R.V. 'Advocate,' which from Wycliffe downwards has

The fourth Gospel alone has the word Paraclete and an express promise of the Paraclete's coming; nevertheless the Synoptic Gospels are not without the hope of such assistance after the Lord's departure. "Ye shall be brought," we read, "before kings and rulers for my sake...whatsoever shall be given you in that hour speak, for it is not ye that speak but the Holy Spirit," "the Spirit of your Father that speaketh in you."[1] This is in effect a promise that the Holy Spirit will after the Lord's withdrawal defend the Church in its conflict with the world. St John has a wider view of the work of the second Paraclete, to which we shall presently come. Meanwhile it is to be noted that the other Paraclete is neither identical with the first, nor of another nature. For 'other' there are in the Greek New Testament two words,[2] of which, according to Bishop Lightfoot,[3] one "adds," while the other "distinguishes"; and it is the first of the two which the Evangelist uses here. The second Paraclete is not the

been used in the Epistle, represents, there can be little doubt, the true meaning in both passages; apart from this, it is a serious misfortune that the different renderings obscure the truth that the Church has now two Advocates, one with the Father, the other with and in ourselves.

[1] Mc. xiii. 9 ff., Mt. x. 19 f.

[2] ἄλλος and ἕτερος. Cf. Lightfoot, *On a Fresh Revision*, p. 74 f. His judgement has been disputed by Sir W. M. Ramsay (*Historical Commentary on Galatians*, 260 ff.), but the last word on the subject has not been spoken. On the use of ἄλλος by St John, see Abbott, *Gr.* 2676 f.

[3] On Gal. I. 6 f.

first, not simply a spiritualized and heavenly Christ; but neither is He a person of a different nature or of other functions. In the words of the later Church, "Such as the Father is, such is the Son, and such is the Holy Ghost,"[1] possessing the same essence, the same fulness of power and wisdom and love, carrying on the same work with the same purpose and for the same end. One Paraclete goes, only to give place to another such as the first was; but with this difference, that He comes to abide. He cannot be put to death, He will not return to the Father; He is given to the Church to abide "for ever," to the end of the present order, through the whole course of history. His province does not lie only in days of persecution when confessors and martyrs need His defence and support; He is with the whole Church to the end of time, for all purposes for which His help is needed. He is "with" us, in the fellowship of spirit with spirit; not among us only, not only co-operating with us,[2] but a living Presence which penetrates our inmost being, sharing our griefs and joys, controlling our passions, conquering our sins, interceding in our prayers, our indwelling Advocate as our Lord is our Advocate with the Father.

Jesus proceeds to identify this second Paraclete.

---

[1] "Qualis Pater, talis Filius, talis et Spiritus Sanctus" (*Quicumque*, 7).
[2] Μεθ' ὑμῶν, not merely παρ' ὑμῖν or even σὺν ὑμῖν.

He is "the Spirit of the Truth." The phrase occurs in this discourse again more than once.[1] We remember the words "I am the Truth," and ask whether "the Spirit of the Truth" is equivalent to the Spirit of Christ. Doubtless, since our Lord is the Truth, the Spirit of the Truth is His Spirit. Yet 'the Spirit of the Truth' connotes more than the relation of the Spirit to the Son. It represents the Spirit of Christ as the Interpreter of all the truth which finds its centre and expression in the Incarnate Word. If Christ is the Truth, it is the Spirit who presents the truth to the conscience of men. "He bears witness to the truth as being the Spirit of it... the voice of the Spirit will be heard only in the interpretation of truth, and specially of the Truth."[2] Thus the phrase sets forth the office of the other Paraclete as witnessing continually in men to all that is true in life and thought. What Christ is, the Spirit of Christ declares.

This promise of the Spirit is made to the disciples of Christ only, and not to the world at large. Why this is so the Lord now explains. *Which* [Spirit] *the world cannot receive, for it doth not behold it, nor know it; ye know it, for it abideth with you and is in you* (xiv. 17 *b*). The world is not capable of seeing the invisible or of knowing that which transcends

[1] xv. 26, xvi. 13. Cf. 1 Jo. iv. 6, v. 6.
[2] Hort, *The Way, the Truth, and the Life*, p. 57.

the intellect. The world, therefore, cannot receive the Spirit; He can be received only by those who know Him because He has already dwelt amongst them and even within them.

This sharp contrast between the disciples of Christ and the world [1] is characteristic of the Fourth Gospel, and especially of the Last Discourse. The Lord came to save the world,[2] but in so far as the world refuses to be saved, it becomes antagonistic to Christ and to God, and this antagonism, present to our Lord's mind from the first, is felt more intensely as the end draws near. The world is ruled by the Great Adversary; it hates Christ and His disciples, and will rejoice over His departure. The Lord does not pray for it in His last intercessory prayer.[3] This hostile world is not susceptible of spiritual influences; under its present condition, the Spirit has no reality in its eyes. The psychic man, as St Paul afterwards spoke, has no capacity for the spiritual; no faculty by which he can acquaint himself with a Person who is pure spirit, who eludes the vision and cannot be apprehended by the intellectual power of man.[4] The world can go no further than its senses or its mental powers carry it, and the Spirit reveals itself to neither. Ultimate realities lie outside the

[1] ὁ κόσμος, as ever in St John, not ὁ αἰών.
[2] iii. 16 ff.   [3] xiv. 30, xv. 18 f., xvi. 20, xvii. 9.
[4] Cf. 1 Cor. ii. 14 ψυχικὸς δὲ ἄνθρωπος οὐ δέχεται τὰ τοῦ πνεύματος τοῦ θεοῦ . . . καὶ οὐ δύναται γνῶναι.

range of its knowledge. It had not recognized the Word, though it was made by Him; nor could it recognize the Spirit, though He has come into it and is at work in the mystery of human life.

On the other hand, the disciples of Christ already had some acquaintance with the workings of the Divine Spirit. "Ye—the pronoun is emphatic[1]—ye, in contrast with the world—know the Spirit, for it dwells among you and is in you." The Lord does not say "Ye behold the Spirit," as He says shortly afterwards "Ye behold me,"[2] but "Ye know it"; you are already learning to acquaint yourselves with the Spirit by experiencing His work. The Spirit which was to be "with" them after the Pentecost already dwelt amongst them in the person of Christ, who had been baptized with the Holy Ghost, and from whom the fulness of the Spirit overflowed in words and acts of grace. But in what sense could He be said to be already "in" them? Has not St John himself told us that there was no outpouring of the Spirit till Jesus was glorified? It was doubtless this that led to the substitution by the great majority of our authorities of "shall be" for "is."[3] But the present suits the context: 'Ye know Him for He is not

[1] ὑμεῖς γινώσκετε αὐτό.

[2] ὑμεῖς δὲ θεωρεῖτέ με (v. 19).

[3] ἐστίν BD*; ἔσται ℵAD², etc. The Vulgate Latin changes both presents into futures: "apud vos manebit (μενεῖ), et in vobis erit (ἔσται)." On ἐστίν see Hare, *Mission of the Comforter*, ii. note 1.

only among you but within you already; your knowledge is based on an experience already begun.' Even before the Pentecost, even while the Lord Jesus went in and out among them, the Spirit was stirring in their hearts; not yet as their Advocate, not in the fulness or ripeness of His gifts, but as imparting so much of spiritual life as enabled them to respond in some measure to the teaching of Christ. What was it but this foretaste of the Spirit in their inner man that inspired them with such faith and love as they already had? that distinguished them from the unbelieving mass of their contemporaries and fellow-countrymen? They knew the Spirit already, not merely as manifested in their Master, but as dwelling in themselves. They could not have put a name to this life within them, of which they were but dimly conscious; but the Master tells them now that it was the presence in them of Him whom they were soon to know as the "other Paraclete, the Spirit of the truth."

## VI.

So completely would the other Paraclete take up and carry on the work of the first that His coming would be a return of Christ Himself to the orphaned Church. *I will not leave you fatherless*, the Lord proceeds; *I am coming to you. Yet a little while, and the world beholdeth me no more, but ye behold me; because I live, ye shall live also* (xiv. 18 f.).

"I will not leave you fatherless." "Comfortless" in the Authorized Version suggests a reference to the "Comforter,"[1] which is entirely wanting in the Greek; "desolate" in the Revised, is an interpretation rather than a rendering of the original, which is simply 'orphans,' or according to the usual acceptation of the word, 'fatherless children.'[2] Jesus had been more than Advocate to the Eleven, He had been the father to whom they had looked for everything; and His departure would leave them orphans, compelled to shift for themselves while they were yet far from maturity. 'But,' He assures them, 'it

[1] As if, instead of ὀρφανούς, the translators had read ἀπαρακλήτους.

[2] For ὀρφανός see Ps. lxvii. 6 (LXX), Tobit i. 8, Sirach iv. 10, 1 Macc. iii. 10, James i. 27.

shall not be so, except for the moment. I will not leave you as a father leaves his children when death tears him from them. You must not think of me as dead, or as really parted from you. I shall be alive, and in touch with you; nay, I am coming to you again, and you shall see me and shall share my life.'

For years the world had looked on the visible form of the Incarnate. The face, the attitude, the look and manner of the Word made flesh, known to us now only through the painter's or the sculptor's art, or by a precarious tradition, were familiar to thousands, as well as to the Twelve. A few hours more and this vision will be taken for ever from the world, the hostile or indifferent majority; but the Church will retain it: "ye (the emphatic pronoun again) behold me" still. The continued sight of the risen and glorified Lord is neither imaginary, nor a vivid memory of the past; it is a spiritual fact which belongs to the life of the spiritual world. The fact is explained by the words that follow: "Because I live, ye shall live also."[1] The Christ that faith reveals to believers is one who is "alive for evermore," and whose risen life reproduces itself in the body of the Church and in every faithful member of it. The new life infused into the heart of the disciple assures him of the truth of the Resurrection and

[1] Or "For I live, and ye shall live also." But, as Westcott points out, the other construction is more after St John's manner: cf. xiii. 14, xiv. 3, xv. 20.

Ascension. Christ lives in him by the Spirit;[1] he lives in the higher sense because Christ lives, and the image of the Living Christ fills the eye of his heart, so that he beholds Him more truly than the world or even the disciples beheld him in the days of His flesh. The Lord speaks of this life in Him as yet future—"ye shall live"; for the disciples in the Upper Room it was still a future experience,[2] although one which would soon begin.

When that day came the Eleven would understand all that He had said about His oneness with the Father on the one hand and with themselves on the other. *In that day ye shall know that I am in my Father, and ye in me, and I in you* (xiv. 20). Already He has taught them that He is in the Father and the Father in Him;[3] that He was also in them and that they were in Him He would teach them shortly;[4] when the Spirit came they would learn the meaning of these sayings which for the time they must take on faith. *Credo ut intellegam* is a principle which is not without justification in the light of Christian experience; spiritual understanding at its best follows and does not precede belief. With regard to the

---

[1] The πνεῦμα τῆς ζωῆς ἐν Χριστῷ Ἰησοῦ (Rom. viii. 2). Cf. Gal. ii. 20.

[2] Note the contrast ἐγὼ ζῶ, ὑμεῖς ζήσετε. With Him life is normal and ever present (Apoc. i. 17 f. εἰμὶ . . . ὁ ζῶν . . . καὶ ἰδοὺ ζῶν εἰμί); the Eleven as yet knew not what life was: "non ex se sed ex illo vivent" (Bengel).

[3] xiv. 11.     [4] xv. 1 ff.

mystery of coinherence which the Spirit will make a matter of knowledge, it will be observed that the Lord does not say, "and ye in the Father, and the Father in you." Our relations with God are not immediate, but mediated through the Son, who alone is in the Father by oneness of essence. "I in them," the Lord says later, in the Prayer, "and thou in me."[1] We are one with Him who is one with God, and thus our union with the Incarnate Son unites us, creatures and sinners as we are, to the very Source of Godhead itself.

This is high doctrine, which the Lord does not expect the Eleven to apprehend as yet. Meanwhile He returns to the practical and perfectly intelligible teaching of verse 15; but in repeating it, He reverses the order. He had said in the earlier verse, "If ye love me, ye will keep my commandments"; now He says, *He who hath my commandments and keepeth them, he it is that loveth me* (xiv. 21*a*). The propositions are equally true; love ensures obedience, and obedience demonstrates love. The new form of the saying has a feature peculiar to itself; "he who hath my commandments" precedes "and keepeth them."[2] "He who hath," who counts the commandments of Christ among his choicest possessions, loving them, as the Psalmist loved the commandments of God "above gold, yea,

[1] xvii. 23.

[2] Aug. *tract. in Joann.* lxxv.: "qui habet in memoria et servat in vita."

above fine gold";[1] he who keeps them, not as a treasure under lock and key, or as a talent hidden in the earth, but by putting them to daily use— this man without any doubt loves Christ. When obedience to Christ is the primary rule of conduct, love to Christ is the principle of life. This test is in the long run infallible, for no weaker motive can endure the constant demand that the Master makes on the loyalty of His disciples.

*But he that loveth me shall be loved by my Father, and I will love him and will manifest to him myself* (xiv. 21 b). If the demand is great which Christ makes upon love, the reward is also great. Love for Christ is an exacting principle, but it has magnificent issues. It wins the love both of the Son and of the Father.[2] The poor human emotion receives an answer of Divine love; the man who can say, "Lord, thou knowest that I love thee," can say also, 'Christ loves me, God loves me, since I love Christ.' Our Lord's return of love is shewn by self-manifestation. "I will manifest to him my very self"; to such a soul I will make myself plain and clear. The verb[3] is used in the sense of giving definite information or instruction,[4] or, followed by a personal pronoun, of self-

[1] Ps. cxix. 127.

[2] Aug. *ibid.*: "quomodo enim nos pater sine filio, aut filius sine patre diligeret? quomodo cum inseparabiliter operentur, separabiliter diligunt?"

[3] ἐμφανίζειν.   [4] Acts xxiii. 15, 22.

presentation. There is a close parallel to the present passage in the prayer of Moses already quoted; for "Shew me now thy ways" becomes in the Septuagint version, "Reveal to me thyself"—make Thyself clearly seen.[1] The same verb is used in Hebrews, where our Lord is said to have entered heaven to "shew Himself before the face of God."[2] As God revealed Himself to Moses when He "made all His goodness pass before him"; as the Incarnate Son now stands revealed in the Father's sight in heaven, so will He reveal Himself even on earth, according to our measure, to all who love Him in truth. It is not of physical or quasi-physical manifestations that He speaks here, though such were granted to the Eleven during the forty days after the Resurrection,[3] nor to visions like those that came to Stephen and Saul and the prophet of the Apocalypse, but of the purely spiritual illumination which is granted in some degree to every believer: the clear impression of the reality of the object of faith which is made upon the soul from time to time as it meditates or prays or communicates. Those who love Christ are justified by His promise in regarding such impressions as real though partial manifestations of Himself. There is a self-presentation of our Lord

[1] Exod. xxxiii. 13 ἐμφάνισόν μοι σεαυτόν. See p. 21.

[2] Heb. ix. 24 ἐμφανισθῆναι τῷ προσώπῳ τοῦ θεοῦ ὑπὲρ ἡμῶν.

[3] Cf. Acts i. 3, and x. 40 ἔδωκεν αὐτὸν ἐμφανῆ γενέσθαι, οὐ παντὶ τῷ λαῷ ἀλλὰ μάρτυσι τοῖς προκεχειροτονημένοις ὑπὸ τοῦ θεοῦ ἡμῖν.

to His true disciples which corresponds to His self-presentation to the Father in the Holiest; the latter is due to the presence of the glorified humanity at the right hand of God, the former to the Spirit of Christ dwelling in the heart and revealing Him there to faith and love.

## VII.

*Judas (not the Iscariot) saith to him, Lord, what has come to pass that thou art about to manifest thyself to us, and not to the world?* (xiv. 22).

Once again the thread of the discourse is broken by a question. Thomas was moved to interrupt the speaker when He said, "Ye know the way"; Philip, when He said again, "Ye know the Father, and have seen Him."[1] And now Judas cannot let pass unquestioned the promise, "I will manifest myself to those that love me." As the Evangelist hastens to explain, the Judas who intervenes here is not the Judas of Kerioth, who had left the room before the discourse began, but another of that name, also one of the disciples, probably the Thaddaeus of St Mark and St Matthew, and the Judas son of James of St Luke.[2] Of this second Judas we know nothing more than may be gathered from the present reference to him. His question seems to reveal a type of mind not very spiritual or far-seeing,

[1] xiv. 5, 8.

[2] Mc. iii. 18, Mt. x. 3, Lc. vi. 16, Acts i. 13 ('Ιούδας 'Ιακώβου).

but essentially loyal to the Master. What had happened[1] to make Him forgo His chance of winning the world to His side by a public manifestation of His power? The problem had long perplexed the Twelve. What was the meaning of the Lord's reserve? Why did He charge those whom He healed not to make Him known? why refuse to assume the title of Messiah? why hide Himself from those who would have made Him king? why limit His self-revelation to a handful of men like themselves? Had He but taken His true place in the life of His time, had He put Himself at the head of a national movement, the whole country would have gone down before Him, and by this time He might have been reigning in Jerusalem, and they, His disciples, seated on His right hand and on His left in His kingdom. His unbelieving brethren had cast in His teeth the inconsistency of His conduct in performing Messianic acts and yet refraining from an open appeal to the support of His countrymen; "if thou doest these things, shew thyself to the world."[2] His disciples had kept their questionings to themselves until now, when the last opportunity of public self-manifestation had been lost, and Jesus declared Himself content to be known and loved by the Eleven. Then at length Judas gave voice to that which was passing in the

[1] τί γέγονεν ὅτι . . . Vulg. "quid factum est quia."
[2] Jo. vii. 4.

minds of all. Something of which they were not cognizant must have led the Lord to adopt this extraordinary policy of revealing Himself only to a dozen poor and uninfluential men, and withholding the sight of His glory from the great world. And this, after all that He had said about the Kingdom of God and the glory of the Son of Man, and the world-wide extension of His Church. Whence this discrepancy between His words and acts?

The Lord does not rebuke this outburst; it was loyal and honest, though ignorant. Nor does He explain His conduct: the time for explanation had not come, and to anticipate it was worse than fruitless. He answers by re-stating, and at the same time carrying a step further His teaching about love and obedience and the reward of both. *Jesus answered and said to him, If any love me, he will keep my word, and my Father will love him; and unto him we will come and make our abode with him* (xiv. 23).

In substance this is a repetition of verses 15, 21; but there are significant changes in detail. "My word" is more comprehensive than "my commandments."[1] The "commandments" of Christ are the specific parts of His message bearing on human conduct; His "word" is His message as a whole,

[1] τὸν λόγον μου (xiv. 23), τὰς ἐντολὰς τὰς ἐμὰς or μου (xiv. 15, 21).

His Gospel. By keeping His commandments His disciples attain to the keeping of His word—to the apprehension and appreciation of His entire message. When the Lord comes to the reward to be given to those who keep His word, there is a still more remarkable developement. "My Father will love him": so much He had said already, but now He adds, "and we will come unto him, and make our abode[1] with him." We—both the Father and the Son—will take up our abode in that man's heart. Christ had spoken of preparing a mansion or abode for His disciples in the Father's House hereafter; now He goes further, and promises that the Father and Himself will come and lodge in them while they are yet on earth. The indwelling of God in men is a favourite thought with St John, and appears more than once in his first epistle. "Herein we know that we abide in Him and He in us, in that He has given us of His Spirit."[2] "Whosoever shall confess that Jesus is the Son of God, God abideth in him, and he in God." St Paul, writing to the inhabitants of Greek cities which were adorned with the shrines of the Greek gods, expresses the same truth in another form: "Your body is a temple of the Holy Spirit that is in you, which ye have from God."[3] The body of a Christian is a sanctuary,

---

[1] $\mu o\nu \grave{\eta} \nu\ \pi a \rho'\ a \mathring{v} \tau \hat{\wp}\ \pi o \iota \eta \sigma \acute{o} \mu \epsilon \theta a.$ On $\mu o\nu \acute{\eta}$ see xiv. 2.
[2] 1 Jo. iv. 13.   [3] 1 Cor. vi. 19.

since God dwells in it by the Holy Spirit. It is thus that we must doubtless understand the great saying of Christ: "We will come to him, and make our lodging with him." The Spirit of the Father and the Son dwells in those who love and obey Christ. And it is by the indwelling of the Spirit that Christ manifests Himself to such.[1]

So far the Lord has answered the first part of Judas's question: the answer to the second is on the same lines: "What has happened that thou wilt not manifest thyself to the world?" 'This, that the world keeps not my word, and therefore cannot receive the indwelling of the Spirit by which I am manifested to those who love me.' *He that loveth me not keepeth not my words*—the utterances of my word; *and the word which ye hear is not mine* in its origin and ultimate source, *but that of the Father who sent me* (xiv. 24). 'To reject or neglect my words is to set at naught not the Son only but the Father from whom I am sent; and for those who do so no revelation of either Father or Son is possible, because there is no place in their hearts for the Spirit of Both, by whom only that inner revelation can be made.'

---

[1] Cf. Apoc. iii. 20 εἰσελεύσομαι πρὸς αὐτόν, καὶ δειπνήσω μετ' αὐτοῦ καὶ αὐτὸς μετ' ἐμοῦ. Augustine's comment (*tract.* lxxvi.) is interesting: "est ergo quaedam Dei manifestatio interior quam prorsus impii non noverunt, quibus Dei patris et Spiritus Sancti manifestatio nulla est, filii vero potuit esse sed in carne."

## VIII.

THE Lord now proceeds to speak of the work of the other Paraclete in the hearts and minds of His disciples. *These things I have spoken to you while abiding with you. But the Paraclete, the Holy Spirit which the Father will send in my name, he shall teach you all things, and remind you of all things that I said to you* (xiv. 25 f.).

The Lord's abode with the Eleven in the flesh[1] was now at an end; and though His words might remain as a permanent heritage for the Church,[2] the familiar human voice would be heard no longer. The teaching of the Ministry was complete. But not all teaching, not every form of communication between Christ and His Church had ceased; intercourse would be carried on through the Paraclete who was to abide with her for ever.

The Paraclete is none other than "the Holy

---

[1] So μένων, qualified by παρ' ὑμῖν, must be understood here; cf. p. 40.

[2] As λελάληκα seems to imply. The perfect is used throughout the Last Discourse (xiv. 25, xv. 3, 11, xvi. 1, 4, 6, 25, 33), except in xv. 22, where the reference is to the hostile Jews; in the earlier chapters of the Gospel it is rare (vi. 63, viii. 40).

Spirit" of the Old Testament,[1] who inspired the prophets and guided the heroes and saints of the older dispensation. But He is now to be sent to the Church in a new capacity, as the Spirit of the Incarnate Son, as representing the glorified Christ, and carrying on His work on earth. He who spake by the prophets will now come to speak in the name of the Son. It is He who will henceforth be the Teacher of the Church, and His teaching will embrace all religious truth,[2] and not only the fragments of truth which had been revealed to Israel in the days before the advent. It will be wider and fuller than the teaching of Jesus, an interpretation of the Lord's teaching which will open it out and fill in the Master's outlines, not, however, superseding them, but rather bringing them back to the memory with new vividness and force. "He[3] shall remind you of all that I[3] said to you." The words fulfil themselves in the Gospels: not that the Gospels, even the Synoptics, have preserved a verbatim report of the sayings of Christ; the same sayings are reported with considerable variations even where two Evangelists are reproducing materials which have been borrowed from a third. But the memoirs, written

[1] Ps. li. 11, Isa. lxiii. 10 f.

[2] Cf. 1 Jo. ii. 27 τὸ αὐτοῦ χρίσμα διδάσκει ὑμᾶς περὶ πάντων.

[3] The pronouns are both emphatic (ἐκεῖνος and ἐγώ), the ἐγώ especially so, standing as the last word of the sentence. Cf. xxi. 13 f.

or oral, which lie behind our present Gospels, had no other foundation than the recollections of the Twelve, or of others who were associated with them.[1] The Eastern memory is proverbially retentive, but it is not unreasonable to suppose that in the case of these men it was quickened by the coming of the Spirit. So at least St John seems to have believed, for twice in his Gospel[2] he notes that forgotten sayings and circumstances came back to the disciples after the Resurrection or Ascension. But this office of the Spirit was assuredly not limited to the first disciples. He is the Teacher of the Church in all ages; each age receives from Him its own lessons of truth, and its own appreciation of the words of Christ. It belongs to Him as the Giver of life to quicken the whole nature of man. No one who has had any experience in pastoral work can fail to recall instances in which the understandings and memories of uneducated Christians have been enabled in a remarkable degree to apprehend and retain profound religious truth, although other branches of knowledge were beyond their reach. Such cases recall Christ's words, and justify the belief that they are operative in our present experience.

The first section of the Last Discourse is drawing to a close. Its purpose has been to still the fears of

[1] "Exemplum praebet haec ipsa homilia" (Bengel).
[2] ii. 22, xii. 16.

the Eleven, who were agitated by the prospect of the Lord's departure. It ends as it began, with words which inspire calm and confidence. *Peace I leave to you, my peace I give you ; not as the world giveth give I to you. Let not your heart be troubled, neither let it play the coward* (xiv. 27).

"Peace to you" was the common greeting to friends on arrival or return.[1] Jesus leaves it as He departs. On His lips the words were not conventional: His peace was no empty form of words, but a substantial gift. As a father leaves his estate to his sons, so the Lord left the Eleven His own peace[2] —that which had kept Him calm and strong in life, and now, in prospect of the Cross, made Him the one person at the supper-table who was not agitated or afraid. There had been moments, indeed, when His peace of mind was shaken;[3] more than one such moment was to come before the end;[4] but the balance was quickly restored by fellowship with God. He bequeaths to those whom He leaves behind a peace such as this : a peace not unbroken, not imperturbable, not the suppression of human emotion, but its regula-

---

[1] Cf. Jo. xx. 19, 26. Similarly, 'Go in peace' was the form of dismissal (1 Sam. i. 17).

[2] εἰρήνην τὴν ἐμήν. Cf. xv. 9 τῇ ἀγάπῃ τῇ ἐμῇ, 11 ἡ χαρὰ ἡ ἐμή, 12 ἡ ἐντολὴ ἡ ἐμή, xvii. 24 τὴν δόξαν τὴν ἐμήν. Phil. iv. 7 may be compared : ἡ εἰρήνη τοῦ θεοῦ (with the variant Χριστοῦ, A) . . . ἐν Χριστῷ Ἰησοῦ.

[3] See on xiv. 1.

[4] Mc. iv. 40, xv. 34.

tion and control by the higher power of faith and hope. Then He repeats, like a refrain, the words of xiv. 1—" Let not your heart be troubled "—adding a further note of warning, " Neither let it play the coward."[1] Trouble, agitation of soul, may be, as it was in Christ, without sin; but not so cowardice, which springs from " little faith," and may end in the utter loss of spiritual[2] life. The cowardly spirit which refuses to face duty can never be of God; the Spirit of God is the spirit of courageous faith, which drives out craven fear.[3]

Once more, and for the last time, the Lord points out that His departure need cause no disquietude, but was rather a ground for rejoicing. *Ye heard that I said unto you, I go my way, and come to you. If ye loved me ye would have rejoiced that I go unto the Father, for the Father is greater than I* (xiv. 28).

It would be selfish as well as cowardly, after His explanations, to continue to lament His departure, since they knew from His own lips whither He was going. His destination, He had told them, was His Father's House: the inconceivable joy and glory of the Divine presence. It must be a most imperfect,

---

[1] μηδὲ δειλιάτω.

[2] Mc. iv. 40 δειλοί ἐστε; οὔπω ἔχετε πίστιν; cf. Mt. viii. 26 τί δειλοί ἐστε, ὀλιγόπιστοι; Apoc. xxi. 8 τοῖς δὲ δειλοῖς καὶ ἀπίστοις . . . τὸ μέρος αὐτῶν ἐν τῇ λίμνῃ.

[3] 2 Tim. i. 7 οὐ γὰρ ἔδωκεν ἡμῖν ὁ θεὸς πνεῦμα δειλίας. Contrast 1 Cor. xvi. 13 στήκετε ἐν τῇ πίστει· ἀνδρίζεσθε.

a most blind and erring love, that grudged Him this, and would detain Him here, when the greatness of the Father's Right Hand lay before Him there.

"For the Father (He adds) is greater than I." In what sense is the Father greater than the Son? "That which we believe of the glory of the Father, the same we believe of the Son ... without any difference or inequality."[1] Must we then limit our Lord's words to His humanity and understand Him to say only, as the *Quicumque* says, that He is "inferior to the Father as touching His manhood"? Of that inferiority there can be no doubt, since His humanity was, like our own, subject to the limitations of a creaturely nature. But is this all that He means? The New Testament, and this Gospel of St John in particular, assign a pre-eminence in the Life of God to the Person of the Father, and therefore an inferiority of place and order to the Person of the Son, even apart from the weaknesses of His flesh. The Father is greater than the Son, inasmuch as He is Father; the Son is inferior, inasmuch as He is Son. All that the Son has is His by the Father's gift; His existence as Son is derived from the Source of Godhead and not self-originate,[2] eternally derived, but derived nevertheless. Equal to the Father as touching His Godhead, He is inferior to the Father

---

[1] Proper Preface for Trinity Sunday.
[2] v. 26.

in regard to His Sonship and mission.[1] The Father had sent the Son, and now the Son was returning to the Source of His mission and of His very Being. Could this be matter for sorrow on the part of those who loved Him?

But why tell them of the impending change? *And now I have told you before it came to pass, that when it has come to pass, you may believe* (xiv. 29).[2] When they saw Him crucified, risen, ascending, the words spoken this night would come back to them, and instead of being staggered by the events, their faith in Him would be confirmed. 'He foresaw it all,' they would say: 'He foretold it, and His words, so incredible, so incomprehensible at the time, have come true; we can doubt Him no more.' He had kept this revelation, however, to the end; it was almost the last of His utterances. *No more shall I speak much with you, for the Ruler of the world is coming; and in me he hath not anything* (xiv. 30). No further

---

[1] The history of the subject is fully examined in Westcott's Additional Note on this verse. It will be sufficient here to quote the summary of the Eastern theology of the subject given by John of Damascus, *de fide orth.* i. 8 εἰ δὲ λέγομεν τὸν πατέρα ἀρχὴν εἶναι τοῦ υἱοῦ καὶ μείζονα, οὐ προτερεύειν αὐτὸν τοῦ υἱοῦ χρόνῳ ἢ φύσει ἀποφαινόμεν ... οὐδὲ καθ' ἕτερόν τι εἰ μὴ κατὰ τὸ αἴτιον· τουτέστιν ὅτι ὁ υἱὸς ἐκ τοῦ πατρὸς ἐγεννήθη καὶ οὐχ ὁ πατὴρ ἐκ τοῦ υἱοῦ, καὶ ὅτι ὁ πατὴρ αἴτιός ἐστι τοῦ υἱοῦ φυσικῶς. Augustine speaks for the West in similar terms (*de fide et symb.* 18): "in quantum filius est de patre accepit ut sit, cum ille de filio id non acceperit ... filius patri debet quod est ... pater autem nulli debet quidquid est."

[2] Cf. xiii. 19, xvi. 4.

opportunities would occur after this night for the long conversations and discourses of past days. That hostile power which the Jews knew as the "Ruler of the World"[1] was coming to renew the awful conflict of Evil with Good, which had been suspended after the Temptation in the Wilderness only to be resumed and finally decided in the Garden and on the Cross.[2]

Then, lest the Eleven should suppose that the issue was doubtful, and find here a fresh cause for alarm, He adds at once that the World-Ruler comes to Him in vain. "In me he hath not anything": no foothold, nothing that he can call or make his own; no sin,[3] no momentary rebellion of the will, nothing on which he can lay hold and say, 'This is mine.' He could bring suffering, shame, and even death; but these things give the Adversary no footing in the inner man; sin only can do this. And in Him there was no sin. The Ruler of the World had at last found a man whom he could not rule, even in the least thing. But he could silence Jesus for the time, and this he would do. Let the Eleven make the most

---

[1] שַׂר הָעוֹלָם, ὁ ἄρχων τοῦ κόσμου τούτου (xii. 31, xvi. 11) or, as here, simply τοῦ κόσμου: see J. Lightfoot on the former passage. The Jews seem to have identified the Ruler of the World with Sammael the Angel of Death, rather than Satan; but see Buxtorf, s.v. סַמָּאֵל, and cf. Heb. ii. 14.

[2] So St Luke (iv. 13): ὁ διάβολος ἀπέστη ἀπ' αὐτοῦ ἄχρι καιροῦ.

[3] Aug. *tract.* lxxix.: "nullum scilicet omnino peccatum ... quia neque cum peccato deus venerat, nec eius carnem de peccati propagine virgo pepererat."

of the brief opportunity that remained; it would be long before they heard His voice again. He adds:

*But* [this will come to pass] *in order that the world may know that I love the Father, and as the Father gave me commandment, so I do* (xiv. 31). The construction is uncertain,[1] but the sense does not greatly differ, however we translate the sentence. If the Lord's victory was sure, since there was in Him nothing on which the Evil one could lay hold, what need was there for Him to submit to the last agony and the Cross? They were necessary as a supreme demonstration before the world of His devotion to the Father, and to fulfil the Divine purpose and the terms of the mission He had received. It was enough for Him to know that the Will of the Father required this final sacrifice. Perhaps it ought to be enough for the Church to share this knowledge; it may be that the failure of every effort to formulate a fully satisfactory doctrine of the Atonement is due to this cause. There is in the Cross something which is beyond our present comprehension, but which, we are assured, finds its explanation in "the good and acceptable and perfect Will of God."

One great section of the Last Discourse is now ended, and with its conclusion there is a change of

[1] Is it ἵνα γνῷ . . . οὕτως ποιῶ, or are the last two words to be connected only with καὶ καθὼς ἐντολήν κ.τ.λ. and are we to understand before ἵνα γνῷ some such words as ταῦτα γέγονεν? The latter is simpler, and therefore in St John more probable.

scene. *Arise*, the Lord says, *let us go hence* (xiv. 31 b).[1] The supper chamber is left, probably after the singing of a 'hymn,' perhaps the Hallel Psalms (cxv.-cxviii.); and, as the Synoptists tell us, the Lord and His disciples "went forth to the Mount of Olives."[2] They did not, it appears, go straight to the Garden, for the crossing of the Kidron followed the Prayer.[3] Nor can it be conceived that the Prayer or the rest of the Discourse was uttered as they passed through narrow and crowded streets of the city, or on the short steep path that led from the city walls to the Kidron. But the way from the Cenaculum[4] to the Garden would take them through the Temple precinct, if the precinct was open so late in the evening, as was probably the case at the Passover season.[5] Here and, as it seems, here only can there have been a fitting scene for the rest of the Discourse and the Prayer. In the vast colonnades of the Court of the Gentiles a

[1] With the form ἐγείρεσθε, ἄγωμεν ἐντεῦθεν compare Mc. xiv. 42 (Mt. xxvi. 46) ἐγείρεσθε, ἄγωμεν. The occasion of course was different; but this way of announcing a move may well be a genuine reminiscence of the Lord's manner.

[2] Mc. xiv. 26 (Mt. xxvi. 30), Lc. xxii. 39.

[3] xviii. 1 ταῦτα εἰπὼν Ἰησοῦς ἐξῆλθεν.

[4] On the position of the Cenaculum see Sanday, *Sacred Sites of the Gospels*, p. 77 ff.

[5] Edersheim, *The Temple*, p. 116. Josephus (cited by Westcott on xvii. 3) says distinctly that at the Passover the temple gates were opened at midnight (*ant.* xviii. 2): τῶν ἀζύμων τῆς ἑορτῆς ἀγομένης . . . ἐκ μέσης νυκτὸς ἐν ἔθει τοῖς ἱερεῦσιν ἦν ἀνοιγνύναι τοῦ ἱεροῦ τοὺς πυλῶνας.

quiet corner could readily have been found where the Discourse might be resumed; the formal abandonment of the precinct the day before [1] does not forbid the supposition that it was used afterwards for private teaching and devotion.

There are those who would transpose the following chapters, placing them before the closing verses of ch. xiii.[2] But the change does violence not only to the textual evidence, but, as we shall see, to the order of the thought. It has been urged, indeed, that there is no connexion between chapters xiv. and xv., as they now stand; the allegory of the Vine strikes a new note, and proceeds on other lines. The sequence, it may be admitted, is not obvious, but it is not the less real because it is subtle. In ch. xiv. Jesus has unfolded the purpose of His departure, and thus calmed the fears of the Eleven. In ch. xv. He proceeds to speak of the life which remains for them when He is gone; of their hidden union with Himself, their conflict with the world, the strength and victory of their faith. There is a break at the end of ch. xiv., and a new division of the subject is started in ch. xv. 1, but the new line of thought arises naturally out of that which has gone before, and is indeed its necessary sequel and complement. The allegory

[1] Mt. xxiii. 38, xxiv. 1.
[2] *e.g.* Wendt, *Gospel according to S. John* (English trans.), p. 101 ff.

of the Vine and the branches forms the text of a second part of the great discourse, in which the note of comfort passes into a call to newness of life, the life of the indwelling, fruit-bearing Spirit of Jesus Christ.

# THE LAST DISCOURSE.

*PART II.*

(ST JOHN xv., xvi.)

ζῇ ἐν ἐμοὶ Χριστός.

I.

As they passed through the streets and lanes of the city the Master and His disciples were silent. When the new shelter was reached, in the half light, as we may suppose, of the Temple colonnades, Jesus resumed His discourse and, somewhat in the manner of the days past, He began with an allegory.[1] *I am the True Vine* (xv. 1 a).

What was it that suggested the image of the Vine? Was it the "fruit of the vine,"[2] of which all had drunk at the Supper? Or the vineyards on the slopes of the Kidron Valley? Or a vine trained up the wall of a neighbouring house? Or, if the Temple precinct was the scene of this part of the Discourse, was it the golden vine which with its clusters of golden grapes stood over the great doors that opened into the Most Holy Place?[3] Or, lastly, was the allegory suggested by nothing that met the eye, but borrowed from the Old Testament, whose Psalmists and Prophets had

[1] Cf. Jo. x. 7-9, 11 ἐγώ εἰμι ἡ θύρα· ἐγώ εἰμι ὁ ποιμὴν ὁ καλός.
[2] Lc. xxii. 18.
[3] Josephus, *ant.* xv. 11. 3 ἄμπελος διετέτατο χρυσῆ τοὺς βότρυας ἀπαιωρουμένους ἔχουσα.

repeatedly used the vine or vineyard to represent the relation in which Israel stood to God? "Thou broughtest a vine out of Egypt," we read; "it took root and filled the land." "Let me sing for my well-beloved a song of my beloved touching his vineyard." "I planted thee a noble vine... how art thou turned into the degenerate plant of a strange vine?" "Son of man, what is the vine more than any tree, the vine-branch which is among the trees of the forest? Behold it is cast into the fire for fuel."[1] Even if the use of this imagery was suggested by some object of sight, it can scarcely be doubted that our Lord had in mind these and other Old Testament references to Israel as the vine of God's vineyard. But in His use of them, what a new complexion He puts on the familiar figure! In the Old Testament Israel is the vine; here it is Himself. 'I'—the emphatic pronoun appears again —'I am the Vine, the True Vine, the ultimate fulfilment of the symbol.[2] The Vine brought out of Egypt and planted on the hills of Canaan, and which filled the land, was a shadow of the true; its ideal is come at last. The root and stock from which comes all the good fruit that is borne, whether in Israel or in Gentile lands, all that is best in human life and

[1] Ps. lxxx. 8, Isa. v. 1, Jer. ii. 21, Ezek. xv. 1 ff. The Maccabean coins carried the figure of a vine which represented Israel.

[2] For this use of $\dot{\alpha}\lambda\eta\theta\iota\nu\dot{o}s$ see i. 9, vi. 32; Heb. viii. 2, ix. 24. Cf. Abbott, *Voc.* 1729.

ST JOHN xv. 1, 2            73

history, is here in my Person, in Emmanuel, God with man in the Incarnate Son.'

*And my Father is the husbandman* (xv. 1 *b*),[1] the tiller of the ground, the grower of the True Vine. God is both the owner[2] and also the cultivator; not only is creation His property, but He Himself works in His vineyard by His Word and His Spirit, an immanent and not only a transcendental Power. And if this is true in the case of Nature, still more is it true of the Kingdom of Grace, of the Church, the mystical body which makes up the fulness of the Christ-Vine.

*Every branch in me, if it bear no fruit, he taketh away, and every one that beareth fruit, he cleanseth it, that it may bear more fruit* (xv. 2). The Tiller of the Vineyard comes round with a pruning-knife which He uses on all the branches, whether fruitful or not. But He uses it with varying aims, and in different manners; the fruitful branches are pruned to make their yield greater; the unfruitful are cut right away, since they do not fulfil the proper function of a vine-branch.

The True Vine in the allegory preserves its unity, though its branches are many. The picture which is placed before us is not that of a vineyard,

---

[1] ὁ γεωργός, as in Mc. xii. 1 and the parallels in Mt. and Lc. The more precise ἀμπελουργός occurs only in Lc. xiii. 7.

[2] Cf. Mt. xx. 1 ἀνθρώπῳ οἰκοδεσπότῃ.

with many vines,[1] but of a single vine. The vine represents the whole Church, considered in regard not to external organization, but to the spiritual life of its many members. Every branch, each local church, each individual member is, as our Lord represents, in Him, whether it bears much fruit or none. Members of Christ, branches of the True Vine, which bear no fruit, are still in Him by the communion of the Sacraments; they have not yet been cut off by the judgement of God or by the act of the Church; and it does not belong to their fellow-members to withdraw from fellowship with them, until in one of these ways the Husbandman's pruning-knife fall. Fall it will on fruitless branches of the vine in God's own time, when they must lose at once their part in Christ and their power of bearing fruit.

For the rest of the branches the knife serves another purpose; it 'cleanses' them.[2] As our agriculturists speak of 'cleaning' the land, so the ancients spoke of 'cleansing' fruit-trees, by freeing them from superfluous growth.[3] Branches in Christ are thus cleansed by whatever tends to concentrate life on the work of fruit-bearing, by removing that which would use up vital force without fulfilling

[1] As in Mc. xii. and Mt. xx.

[2] There seems to be a play upon αἴρει, καθαίρει.

[3] So Philo, *de agric.* 2 διὰ ταύτης τῆς γεωργικῆς καὶ ὅσα παθῶν ἢ κακιῶν δένδρα ἀναβλαστόντα εἰς ὕψος ἐξήρθη . . . ὑποτεμνόμενα καθαίρεται.

the great purpose of their union with Christ. The 'cleansed' or pruned branch may emerge from the process lopped and bare, but it has the promise of larger or more abundant fruit in the years to come. Such treatment is not a token of the Divine displeasure, but of the Divine love;[1] it is the reward of some fruit-bearing, and the earnest of more. So the great Husbandman of the True Vine chastens us for our profit, that we may be partakers of His holiness.

As for the Eleven, this work of the Husbandman had been in part anticipated. *Ye*, the Lord says, *are already clean because of the word which I have spoken to you* (xv. 3). During the Ministry the teaching of Christ had served as the pruning-knife; with a wholesome severity it had cut away much of their worldliness and self-seeking. They were not now the men they had been three years ago, but better and purer; in principle and motive they were relatively clean,[2] all except Judas,[3] and Judas had been taken away; the rest were eager to serve the Master better in the time to come, to bear more fruit. But that they might bear more, that they might continue to bear any, one thing was needful; they must abide in the Vine and the Vine in them by a mutual relation. *Abide*

---

[1] Cf. Heb. xii. 5 f., Apoc. iii. 19 f.

[2] Aug. *tract.* lxxx.: "mundi scilicet atque mundandi; quis est enim in hac vita sic mundus ut non sit magis magisque mundandus?"

[3] Cf. xiii. 10 ff. ὑμεῖς καθαροί ἐστε, ἀλλ' οὐχὶ πάντες κ.τ.λ.

*in me, and I in you* (xv. 4 *a*). No pruning would suffice without the maintenance of this vital union between the Vine and its branches. The Lord does not say, 'Come unto me,' or 'Join yourselves to me,' for they were already in Him, as branches in the tree; by His choice of them, and their faith in Him, He and they were one. Yet the union must not only be formed, it must be maintained, they continuing to live in Him, He continuing to pour His life into them; each side in this reciprocal activity being essential to the other, and guaranteeing the action of the other. But whereas the Vine cannot fail to do its part, the branch may easily cease to remain in vital union with the Vine, and in that case it ceases to bear fruit. And *as the branch cannot bear fruit of itself unless it abide in the vine, so neither can ye* bear fruit *unless ye abide in me* (xv. 4 *b*). Even when 'cleansed' the branch has no inherent vitality, no independent productivity;[1] the husbandman's pruning-knife secures fruitfulness only so long as the branch coheres with the vine. Exactly so it is with the branches of the True Vine. They have no power of themselves to bear fruit unto holiness, and no Divine discipline will give it to them, unless they maintain their inner union with Jesus Christ, and thus draw spiritual life and nourishment from the root.[2]

[1] Augustine: "ut responderet futuro Pelagio."
[2] Cf. Hosea xiv. 9 ἐξ ἐμοῦ ὁ καρπός σου εὕρηται.

## ST JOHN xv. 4, 5

External union without faith and love leaves the soul barren and dead.

The allegory is now explained and applied to the Eleven. *I am the Vine, ye are the branches.*[1] *He that abideth in me and I in him, he it is that beareth much fruit; for apart from me ye can do nothing* (xv. 5). Whatever checks intercourse between the Lord and His members, in that proportion diminishes the fruit of the Spirit, which depends on the maintenance of vital union with Christ. If the separation is complete, spiritual atrophy and powerlessness ensue; if communion is fully maintained, the fruit is abundant. As in the first creation, "not one single thing was made apart from" the pre-existent Word,[2] so in the new creation of the Spirit no spiritual process is carried on, and no spiritual fruit is produced, apart from the Incarnate Word. But the only alternative to a state of separation from Christ is to abide in Him, to keep our sacramental union with Him alive and active by the exchanges of a constant fellowship, drawing ever fresh supplies from Him and "grace for grace." And this means constant effort. The natural branches draw nourishment from the tree automatically; the branches of the True Vine, as moral beings, maintain or abandon this union with the Vine at pleasure, and thus

[1] As Augustine acutely remarks: "unius naturae sunt vitis et palmites."

[2] Jo. i. 3 χωρὶς αὐτοῦ ἐγένετο οὐδὲ ἕν: cf. xv. 5 χωρὶς ἐμοῦ οὐ δύνασθε ποιεῖν οὐδέν.

are severally responsible for the measure of fruitfulness which each of them attains.

What happens to souls that do not abide in Christ and therefore bear no fruit? The Lord anticipates this question and answers it beforehand. *If a man abide not in me, he is cast out like a branch, and is withered; and men gather them together and cast them into the fire, and they are burned* (xv. 6). We see the labourers in the vineyard following the steps of the husbandman. The ground is strewn with the dead and dying wood which has been cut away from the vine. But it is not left there for long. Busy hands gather it up, bind it in bundles, and cast it out of the vineyard,[1] which now comes into sight; out on the waste land beyond we see a fire kindled and smoke rising, and we hear the crackling of the not yet sapless branches as they feel the heat.[2] It is our wisdom not to press for an exact interpretation of every feature of this picture or of the corresponding harvest scene of Matt. xiii. 40 ff. But there are a few points which it is impossible to overlook or greatly misunderstand. Both pictures represent the final removal from the Church whether by excommunication or death or by personal choice of those who have abandoned their faith in Christ:

[1] ἐβλήθη ἔξω.

[2] Cf. Ezek. xv. 4 πυρὶ δέδοται εἰς ἀνάλωσιν, τὴν κατ' ἐνιαυτὸν κάθαρσιν ἀπ' αὐτῆς (sc. τῆς ἀμπέλου) ἀναλίσκει τὸ πῦρ. With καίεται cf. Exod. iii. 2 ὁ βάτος καίεται πυρί, ὁ δὲ βάτος οὐ κατεκαίετο.

the binding together in a hideous fellowship of barrenness and spiritual death of souls which once were in union with the True Vine; the unprofitableness of Christian lives which through their own fault have been finally abandoned by the Giver of life. The disciple of Christ must choose between this end and the maintenance of his union with the Lord: *aut vitis aut ignis*, as Augustine tersely says—either he is a fruit-bearing branch in the Vine or he becomes fuel for the fire that consumes the refuse for which God has no place in His new world. The vine-branch cut away from the vine can serve no useful purpose;[1] its "end is to be burned."[2]

[1] Ezek. xv. 5 ff.   [2] Heb. vi. 8 τὸ τέλος εἰς καῦσιν.

## II.

The Lord now turns to the bright alternative. *If ye abide in me, and my sayings abide in you, ask*[1] *whatsoever ye will, and it shall be done for you* (xv. 7).

The result of abiding in Christ is not simply that we bear fruit unto God; it brings its reward in the growing freedom and success of our prayers. "If ye abide in me"; the Lord does not now add "and I in you," but "and my sayings abide in you." He substitutes a tangible proof of His presence in us for the presence itself. His "sayings" are the principles of truth and life which constitute His "word";[2] to have them abiding in us is to be loyal to His teaching, and to be guided by it in detail—the surest sign of the presence of His Spirit in our hearts. We ask what we will if our will is in accordance with the will of Christ, which is one with the will of God. There is thus a close connexion between life and prayer; conformity to the mind and will of Christ at once enlarges the scope of our petitions and secures their

---

[1] αἰτήσασθε BADL, αἰτήσεσθε ℵEG.

[2] For the contrast between ῥήματα (xv. 7) and λόγος (xv. 3) cf. xiv. 10, 23 f.

## ST JOHN xv. 7, 8

fulfilment. The reason for this is not far to seek: in Dr. Westcott's words, "the petitions of the true disciples are echoes (so to speak) of Christ's words... their prayer is only some fragment of His teaching transformed into a supplication, and so it will necessarily be heard." It will not escape those who closely follow the teaching of the Prayer-book how many of the Collects and other prayers of the Church are based directly on the " words " of Christ or of Scripture.

*In this* (the Lord continues) *is my Father glorified that ye bear much fruit, and become*[1] *my disciples* (xv. 8) The success of their prayers is not the highest aim set before the members of Christ. It is much to be at liberty to ask whatever we will and to receive it; but it is more to be permitted to bear much fruit, and to glorify God. *Ad maiorem Dei gloriam* was the ultimate purpose even of the Master;[2] the disciple proves his claim to that title in so far as he too brings glory to the Father of our Lord Jesus Christ. And this he does if he abides in the Son, and brings forth in abundance the fruit of the Spirit of Christ. So he becomes a disciple indeed, learning to be as Christ was.[3] True discipleship is hardly begun till the earthly life is near its end, and the fruit hangs thick and ripe upon the branches of the Vine ; " now,"

---
[1] γένησθε BDL, γενήσεσθε ℵAEG.   [2] Cf. xiv. 13, xvii. 2, 4.
[3] Eph. iv. 20 ἐμάθετε τὸν χριστόν.

exclaims Ignatius more than once upon his way to martyrdom, "now I begin to be a disciple." [1]

*As the Father loved me, I also loved you; abide in my love* (xv. 9).

The Lord again varies the terms of His appeal to His disciples to abide in Him: "abide ye in my love."[2] He had loved them with a love which bore some analogy to the Divine love of the Father for the Son. The Father loved the Son before the foundation of the world; the Son loved His own which were in the world, and loved them to the end. There is no uncertainty, no variableness in either love. But the disciples' answer to the love of the Son was liable to change. One of the Twelve had forsaken Him already; would the Eleven "also go away"?[3] There is eager, almost passionate, entreaty in the appeal, "Abide ye in my love." It is more than "Abide in me"; the earlier injunction calls for the life of faith by which men remain in living union with the Lord; the later adds to this a demand for a love answering to Christ's love for themselves. "The love that is mine" is the precise form of the phrase,[4] and it suggests that our response to the love of Christ should be akin to His, to that love with which He

---

[1] Ign. *Eph.* 3 νῦν ἀρχὴν ἔχω τοῦ μαθητεύεσθαι: *Rom.* 5 νῦν ἄρχομαι μαθητὴς εἶναι.

[2] xvii. 24, xiii. 1.   [3] vi. 67.

[4] τῇ ἀγάπῃ τῇ ἐμῇ: cf. note on xiv. 27.

Himself responds to the love of the Father and goes forth towards His own. "Not only live in me, as I live in you," the Lord would say, "but love me as I loved you; lose not the great gift of my love by neglecting to answer it."

This brings us back to what had been said before as to the sayings of Christ abiding in us. *If ye keep my commandments, ye shall abide in my love; as I have kept my Father's commandments, and abide in his love* (xv. 10). To abide in Christ's love may appear too high and mystical an aim to be realized in common life, and it may be asked with reason what such words mean when translated into terms of ordinary human conduct. The Lord answers this question: to abide in His love means to keep His commandments. This answer may seem to lower the standard set up in the previous verse, and even to recede from a fundamental principle of the kingdom of heaven. It surely cannot be that our Lord here represents Himself as a mere enacter of external rules, or that He regards the performance of particular actions as equivalent to the interior disposition of love. The disposition of love, He teaches, is manifested by the steady effort to fulfil His known will, even when the disciple cannot yet say with St Peter, "Thou knowest that I love thee."[1] Since love alone produces a true obedience, obedience is evidence of

---

[1] xxi. 15 f. σὺ οἶδας (17 σὺ γινώσκεις) ὅτι φιλῶ σε.

love. It is more; it has the promise of a continuance of the Master's love toward the obedient: "Ye shall abide in my love." To turn Christ's command into a promise the disciple has but to persevere in the effort to do as He bids. To know whether he loves the Lord, and is loved by Him, the plain Christian needs only to ask his conscience whether he makes it his daily aim to walk as Christ walked.

Again[1] the Lord points out the correspondence between the Father's relation to Himself, and His own relation to believers. The whole of this reciprocation of obedience and love finds its analogy in His own experience: "as I have kept my Father's commandments and abide in His love." As the love of the Father and the Son is the prototype of the Incarnate Son's love for those whom the Father has given Him, so the obedience of the Son to the Father's will is the model of the obedience which the Son calls us to render to Himself. At the end of His earthly life the Incarnate can say, "I have kept[2] my Father's commandments"; and He holds up His perfect obedience as the pattern of that which we owe to Him. To the Eleven, who had been eye-witnesses of His life, the appeal was incomparably strong. It was as if the Lord had said, "You have seen me from day to

---

[1] See xiv. 20.

[2] τετήρηκα—the keeping is complete, and its results are permanent. Cf. St Paul's τετήρηκα in 2 Tim. iv. 7.

day fulfilling the Father's will; with the same persistence, the same whole-heartedness I would have you now go forth into the world to fulfil mine. It was my meat and drink to do His will and finish His work. And now it is done and my obedience is complete, except for the final act of death, and I leave my example as the model and inspiration of your love. But with this difference: my obedience was rendered directly to the Father, who sent me; yours is to be rendered to me, who am your way to the Father. It is my will that you must obey, my love in which you must abide; that obeying me and abiding in me, you may through me attain to God."

This was a hard saying, a call to imitate the inimitable; the mere attempt to fulfil it would involve constant labour and sacrifice. But it would also bring them joy, such as that which the Lord's life of obedience had brought to Himself. *These things I have spoken unto you, that my joy may be in you and your joy may be made full* (xv. 11).

The purpose of the Lord's now completed[1] teaching had been, not to impose new burdens on His disciples, but to bring them joy; to fill up the measure of their joy by imparting to them that which was peculiarly His own.[2] Had He, then, a secret spring of joy with which no stranger intermeddled? Only once in the

[1] As λελάληκα perhaps implies: see note on xiv. 25.
[2] ἡ χαρὰ ἡ ἐμή: see note on xiv. 27, and cf. xvii. 13.

Gospels is He said to have "rejoiced in spirit";[1] yet underneath the gravity of a face marred more than any man's by the sorrows of life, there was a deep well of the truest joy, the joy of perfect obedience and whole-hearted sacrifice, together with the prospect of the still greater "joy set before Him" in the fruits of His Passion.[2] This joy He desired to impart to His disciples; it would be theirs in proportion as they followed His example, until they were filled with it according to their measure. If Christ's joy is beyond our attainment, our joy may nevertheless through faith in His words be filled to the extent of our capacity. Our nature is satisfied if it is as full of the purest joy as it can hold. This is what the Lord desires and wills to give those who respond to His call. It is His own joy He gives, so far as they can receive it. He does not exclude other joys—the joy of health, of physical or intellectual power, of knowledge, of human love, for which He Himself has made our nature yearn. But to these He adds the joy of service and sacrifice, as that without which all other joys are incomplete; and He speaks from personal knowledge, for that supreme source of joy was peculiarly His own.

[1] Lc. x. 21 ἠγαλλιάσατο τῷ πνεύματι τῷ ἁγίῳ.

[2] Heb. xii. 2 ἀντὶ τῆς προκειμένης αὐτῷ χαρᾶς ὑπέμεινεν σταυρόν. Cf. Mt. xxv. 21, 23 εἴσελθε εἰς τὴν χαρὰν τοῦ κυρίου σου.

## III.

*This is my commandment, that ye love one another, as I loved you* (xv. 12).

The Lord now specifies one of His commandments which comes next after that of love to Himself. He had given it to the Eleven for the first time that evening :[1] it was still a " new commandment," though before the end of the century it had become so familiar, so deeply implanted in the life of the Church, that St John could say it was not new but old.[2] With the new commandment the Lord gave a new motive, His own example—" As I loved you " ; and this also He now repeats. It is noteworthy how often St Paul urges the same reason for brotherly love : " receive one another, as Christ also received us ; forgive one another, as God also in Christ forgave you " ; " walk in love, as Christ also loved us, and delivered Himself as an offering for you " ; " husbands, love your wives, as Christ also loved the Church."[3] In these frequent references to the love of God in

[1] See xiii. 34.
[2] 1 Jo. ii. 7 οὐκ ἐντολὴν καινὴν γράφω ὑμῖν, ἀλλ' ἐντολὴν παλαιάν.
[3] Rom. xv. 7, Eph. iv 32, v. 2, 25.

## THE LAST DISCOURSE

Christ we see how the Great Example worked upon Christian society in the first age, dominating the conduct of Christians everywhere, and tending towards the transfiguration of human life, which was the ultimate purpose of our Lord's mission.

Jesus adds the greatest instance of His love, the death of the Cross, which a few hours would consummate. *Greater love hath none than this, that one lay down his life for his friends* (xv. 13). St Paul seems to speak as if the love of the Cross reached even a higher plane, when he writes: " Scarcely for a righteous man will one die; ... while we were yet sinners Christ died for us";[1] and his estimate is doubtless true. Even the friends of Christ were enemies till He made them friends,[2] and could not have been numbered among His friends had they not been reconciled to God by the death of His Son. As for the Eleven, the Gospels shew, and their own consciences must have told them, how imperfect and unworthy their friendship was; how often they had provoked Him by unbelief or stupid ignorance. Their countless faults must have jarred upon the sinless humanity of the Lord far more than graver sins jar upon ourselves. Friendship such as theirs had not deserved so well of Him as to call for the sacrifice of His life on their behalf.

[1] Rom. v. 7 f.
[2] Rom. v. 10 ἐχθροὶ ὄντες κατηλλάγημεν: cf. Rom. viii. 7 τὸ φρόνημα τῆς σαρκὸς ἔχθρα εἰς θεόν.

He had called them "friends"; He was about to prove His friendship for them by the greatest proof that love could give. Let them for their part justify the title He had given them. *Ye are my friends if ye do that which I command you* (xv. 14). Abraham had been called "the friend of God,"[1] and the name still clings to the father of the faithful in his modern Arabic title El Khalil. The Alexandrian writer of the Book of Wisdom realizes that the honour of a Divine friendship may be shared by later ages; the Wisdom of God, he teaches, passing into holy souls in all generations, makes them "friends of God and prophets."[2] The Lord now bids His disciples claim and make good their great position as friends of Christ. Hitherto they had thought of themselves as His servants, and He had encouraged this view of their relation to Him. It appears in the parables which describe the intercourse of Christ with Christians, and in such sayings as "It is sufficient for the servant that he be as his lord";[3] and this very evening He had affirmed it again in the words, "Ye call me 'The Teacher,' and 'The Lord'; and ye say well, for so I am."[4] But now He substitutes 'friends' for 'servants,' and gives a reason for this change of designation: *I call you 'servants' no longer, for the servant knoweth not what his master is doing; but I have spoken*

---

[1] See 2 Chron. xx. 7, Isa. xli. 8, James ii. 24 φίλος θεοῦ ἐκλήθη.
[2] Wisdom vii. 27.   [3] Mt. x. 25.   [4] Jo. xiii. 13.

*of you as 'friends,' for all things that I heard from my Father I made known to you* (xv. 15).

Why are the servants of Christ so suddenly converted into His friends?[1] There has been no change in the Eleven themselves to justify this new honour. But the time had come for it on other grounds. The Lord has now completed His personal teaching and training of these first disciples; and in so doing He has taken them into His confidence, and has committed to them His secret—all that He Himself had learned from the Father. Thus He has lifted them out of the condition of menial service, and raised them gradually into that of the friends of the Messianic King.[2] Much might still be, much in fact still was obscure to them because imperfectly apprehended; yet the mystery of the Kingdom of God, which was hidden from the rest of the world, had already been given into their hands.[3]

"All things that I heard from my Father" is a phrase used in the Fourth Gospel to signify the whole message which the Son brought to the world.[4] It is not a message for an inner circle of disciples

---

[1] Aug. *tract.* lxxxv.: "potest esse servus et amicus qui servus est bonus."

[2] The ministers and other intimates of an oriental king were known as his "friends" ($\phi i \lambda o \iota$): see Esther v. 10, 14, vi. 15; Dan. iii. 91 (24) ($\tau o \hat{\iota} s \phi \iota \lambda o \iota s$ LXX = $\tau o \hat{\iota} s \mu \epsilon \gamma \iota \sigma \tau \hat{a} \sigma \iota \nu$ Th.); and so frequently in the Books of the Maccabees.

[3] Mc. iv. 11.   [4] Mc. iv. 22, Mt. x. 27.

only; the Father's voice speaks in Christ to all mankind. Nothing had been communicated to the Eleven which they were not eventually to communicate to the whole creation: "there is nothing hid," the Lord taught them, "save that it should be manifested"; "what ye hear, dropt into the ear, that proclaim on the housetops."[1] But meanwhile it was Christ's secret and theirs; and to have been made the first depositories of the revelation was at once the reward of faithful service, and the proof of the Master's friendship.

If we ask how these men came to occupy for the time the exclusive position of friends, confidants, and representatives of Christ, the Lord Himself explains that in the last resort this was due not to themselves, but to Him: *It was not you that chose me, but I that chose you, and appointed you that ye should go your ways and bear fruit, and your fruit should remain* (xv. 16).

The selection of the Twelve was Christ's own act, and it was made with singular care and deliberation. The night before was spent in prayer.[2] There were two stages in the process: first, the Lord "called whom he would," and then from these He "appointed twelve."[3] Into the reasons of His choice we need

---

[1] viii. 26, 40, 47, xiv. 24.   [2] Lc. vi. 12.

[3] Mc. iii. 13 f. προσκαλεῖται οὓς ἤθελεν αὐτός . . . καὶ ἐποίησεν δώδεκα. On the whole subject see Latham, *Pastor pastorum*, p. 238 ff.; Hort, *Ecclesia*, c. ii.

not enter here; the point to which He calls attention is that the choice was His. The Church began with a selection, and the selection depended solely on the Master's will. This fact is emphasized in the discourses of the fourth Gospel [1] in order to impress on the disciples the thought that their relation to Jesus Christ began not with themselves but with Him. As they could not bear fruit of themselves, apart from Christ, so apart from Him they could not have begun to be His disciples, His Apostles, His friends. 'Not you, but I,' is the lesson He would teach—a lesson which it was given to St Paul to carry a step further in his doctrine of the Divine election of the whole Church. The freedom of the human will is not excluded either by our Lord's teaching or by St Paul's. In some sense the Apostles themselves chose Christ for their Master, and all believers do likewise; but neither in the case of the Apostles nor in our own did the choice originate with men. God is before us in all things; all that is good in men comes from Him as its ultimate Source.

Christ's choice of the Twelve laid upon them a great responsibility; with their election to a high office there came their appointment to fulfil its duties. "He appointed twelve"—so St Mark or possibly St Peter comments—"to be with Him, and that He might send them forth to preach."[2] The appoint-

[1] vi. 70, xiii. 18.     [2] Mc. iii. 14.

ment involved two things: (1) the training which was to be gained by association with the Master, and (2) the active work of the mission which was to follow. Of these the first was now over, and on this last night of His life and of their preparation the Lord dwells on the second. The time had come to make proof of their ministry, their Apostleship; to go their ways into the world and bear fruit—both the fruit of holy living and the special fruit of Apostolic service—fruit which would remain after they and their generation had passed away.

Where are we to look for this permanent fruit of the work of the original Apostolate? So far as we can judge, their personal work was not commensurate with the labour bestowed on them by the Lord. Apart from what we learn in the Acts about the early ministrations of St Peter and St John, there are few certain traces of the ways they went or the fruit they bore.[1] The honour of setting on foot the conversion of the Gentile world belongs not to the original Twelve, but to another of the 'friends' of Christ, chosen after His departure from the world. Perhaps we have not sufficient materials for a complete answer to the question. But on the lowest estimate the Eleven accomplished a work which none but the eye-witnesses of the Incarnate life could have done, and of which we reap the fruit to-day. Our

[1] The legends are summarized by Eusebius, *H.E.* iii. 1.

knowledge of the acts and words of Jesus is due to their transmission of the facts as they remembered them. It may be that not one of our four Gospels was written by an Apostle; yet without the witness of the Apostles they could not have been written at all. Our baptismal creed was not composed by the Twelve; yet it rightly bears their name, since it embodies the traditions of their teaching. The Catholic Church in which we believe is Apostolic, inasmuch as it keeps unbroken the fellowship which the Apostolic college initiated. Thus in Canon and Creed and Church the fruit of the Apostles' ministry remains amongst us to this day.

The Eleven themselves, the Lord continues, will reap the fruit of their service in answers to their prayers: *that whatsoever ye shall ask* the Father in my name, *he may give it you* (xv. 16 *b*). This promise has been made already to those who abide in Christ, and in whom His words abide[1]; it is now made to those who bear fruit which remains. There is no essential difference between the two conditions. Abiding in Christ issues in fruitfulness, and fruitfulness is rewarded by new gifts of grace, larger answers to prayer. The Christian life is a complex whole, so compacted together that it cannot be broken up into portions of which some may be claimed and others left. Men cannot pray with success unless

[1] xiv. 13 f., xv. 7.

their life is fruitful, or bear fruit unless they maintain their union with Christ, or maintain that union unless they pray and bear fruit. That which was true herein for the Eleven is true for all members of the Church. Incidentally we learn something as to the normal order of Prayer. We pray to the Father in Christ's name: we receive the answer from the Father. Yet we receive it through the Son, and by the action of the Son; " I," our Lord elsewhere says, " will do it."[1] The Father is so one with the Son, and the Son with the Father, that what the Father gives the Son gives likewise. There is a difference only in the manner of the gift; the Father is the Source, the Son the medium, of every answer to our prayers.

[1] xiv. 14.

## IV.

*These things I command you, that ye may love one another. If the world hateth you, ye know that it hateth me before you. If ye were of the world, the world would have loved its own; but because ye are not of the world, but I chose you out of the world, for this cause the world hateth you* (xv. 17-19).

'The aim of these instructions,'[1] the Lord would say, 'is to stir you to mutual love by the example and after the measure of my love for you. Love from those who are not your fellow disciples you must not expect, nor can you wonder if they meet you with positive hatred. If you find (as you already begin to do[2]) that you are the object of general aversion, call to mind that so also was I.' In the Master's case the world's hatred had reached its climax; it could not pursue Him beyond the grave. The Master would be the first to suffer,[3] but by no means the last. Himself the Protomartyr, He would have a goodly following

---

[1] Namely, those from xv. 11 onwards.
[2] εἰ . . . μισεῖ, not ἐὰν μισήσῃ.
[3] See *The Christian Year*, Hymn for St Stephen's Day.

## ST JOHN xv. 17-19

in all ages, and of many types, victims of the world's hatred for Christ and those who are Christ's.

Whence this rooted dislike? It was to be explained by a radical difference of character. Friendship can exist only between those who are fundamentally at one; the world could not be expected to love any but its own. But the friends of Christ were not merely not of the world; they had been chosen out of it, formed into a body which was in sharp contrast with it and by its very existence condemned and opposed it. That they belonged to Christ was a sufficient reason for expecting that the world would be hostile. He had been in the world, but never of it, and did not hesitate to proclaim His attitude towards it; "ye," He said to the Jews, "are from below, I am from above; ye are of this world, I am not of this world."[1] This 'other-worldliness' He had impressed upon His disciples; "they are not of the world," He says again, "even as I am not of the world."[2] There was in them, as there was in Him, that which the world could neither understand nor forgive. The world loved its own,[3] that which in speech and temper was homogeneous with itself; it could not love, it could not but hate those who had forsaken it to follow a Master whose ideals were exactly opposite to its own. The quarrel of the world with

---

[1] viii. 23.      [2] xvii. 14.
[3] τὸ ἴδιον: cf. viii. 44 ἐκ τῶν ἰδίων λαλεῖ.

the Church, so far as it is not provoked by the faults of Christians, is merely a continuation of its quarrel with Christ. The world complains loudly of the *odium theologicum*, but the *odium saeculare*, the bitterness with which the Church is assailed by the world, far exceeds it. The fact should neither surprise nor distress those who follow in the steps of Christ.[1]

*Remember* (the Lord proceeds) *the word that I said to you, There is no servant greater than his lord. If they persecuted me, they will persecute you also ; if they kept my word, they will keep yours also* (xv. 20).

The saying referred to occurs more than once in the Lord's earlier teaching. It finds a place in His charge to the newly chosen Apostles, and was repeated after the washing of their feet on the last evening of His life.[2] 'Remember' probably looks back to the former of these occasions. From the very first they had been given to understand that fellowship with the Lord would entail participation in His sufferings; for how could they expect to fare better than their Master? Hitherto indeed He had stood between them and the ill-will of the world, and borne

---

[1] See Hobhouse, *The Church and the World*, for the history of the subject ; and for an early appreciation of the fact cf. *ep. ad Diogn.* 6o Χριστιανοὶ ἐν κόσμῳ οἰκοῦσιν οὐκ εἰσὶ δὲ ἐκ τοῦ κόσμου . . . μισεῖ καὶ Χριστιανοὺς ὁ κόσμος μηδὲν ἀδικούμενος, ὅτι ταῖς ἡδοναῖς ἀντιτάσσονται.

[2] Mt. x. 24, Lc. vi. 40, Jo. xiii. 16.

in His own person the fury of its attack; but when He had gone, it would fall upon His followers—let them not doubt this. Thus with perfect frankness the Lord sets before His friends the consequences of their friendship, not in any respect glozing over the unattractive prospect, but forewarning them of the worst that could come, and bidding them prepare for it.[1] He had done so from the first, and now at the end repeats His words. They would recall what He had said when they saw Him on the Cross, and expected to suffer the same death. Their flight from Gethsemane, Peter's eager denials in the palace of the High Priest, the bolted doors on Easter night, shew that they took the warning to heart. It aroused their fears, and for the moment it paralysed them; but it did not shake their loyalty; not one of them returned to the world, but the son of perdition.

*However, all these things they 'will do to you for my name's sake, because they know not him that sent me* (xv. 21). Another reminiscence of the charge given to the newly chosen Apostles. "Ye shall be hated by all (the Lord had then said) for my name's sake."[2] It would support them under unmerited suffering to know that they were hated because they belonged to Christ, and were carrying on

---

[1] Even in a passage (Mc. x. 29 ff.) which seems to hold out the hope of earthly reward the Lord is careful to add μετὰ διωγμῶν.

[2] Mt. x. 22.

## THE LAST DISCOURSE

His work. That this was so in fact is shewn by the records of the Apostolic Church. Peter and John, flogged before the Sanhedrin, went away "rejoicing that they were counted worthy to be put to shame for His Name."[1] Later on St Peter writes to the churches of Asia Minor, "If ye are reproached for the name of Christ ye are happy ... if [any of you] suffer as a Christian, let him not be ashamed."[2] The messages in the Apocalypse to the churches of Asia point to the same secret source of strength and victory; the church of Ephesus had suffered for the name of Christ; the church of Pergamos was holding fast His name; the church of Philadelphia under sore trial had not denied it.[3] In the persecutions of the second and third centuries it was "the Name" that the heathen hated, and in which the Christians gloried.[4]

To know that they suffered for the name of Christ was in itself enough to uphold all true disciples. But consolation might be found also in another thought. The hatred of the world for Christ and Christians was due to ignorance. "Ye neither know me nor my Father";[5] so Jesus had said to the Jews, who

---

[1] Acts v. 40 f.   [2] 1 Peter iv. 14-16.   [3] Apoc. ii. 3, 13, iii. 3.

[4] See *e.g.* Tertullian, *Apol.* 2: "illud solum expectatur quod odio publico necessarium est, confessio nominis: cf. *ibid.* 1: neminem pudet, neminem paenitet ... si denotatur, gloriatur ... interrogatus, vel ultro confitetur."

[5] viii. 19.

professed a unique knowledge of God. If the Jewish leaders knew not God, there were none who did; heathen nations would certainly be little likely to recognize the Divine as manifested in the person of Christ. The character of Jesus was not such as they would associate with their conception of Deity: meekness, humility, love, and sacrifice, finding their consummation in suffering and the death of the Cross, were, from the pagan point of view, incompatible with Divine power and glory. In the Christian virtues the heathen saw, not an interpretation of God, but the extreme of human weakness and folly.[1] Their ignorance of the Father blinded them to the glory of the Incarnate Son, and its reflexion in the new life of the Church. What they said and did against the Church was said and done from ignorance of God, and in this ignorance the Church might find ground for the hope that the world itself, when it came to know the truth, would cease to persecute, and join the company of the friends of Jesus Christ.

[1] See *e.g.* the criticisms of Celsus (Glover, *The Conflict of Religion*, p. 241 f.).

## V.

*If I had not come and spoken to them, they would not have had sin. But now they have no excuse for their sin; he that hateth me, hateth my Father also* (xv. 22 f.).

The ignorance of the heathen world had some excuse. Pilate's soldiers knew not what they did, when they crucified the Lord of Glory;[1] nor did pagan officials such as Trajan and Pliny, or the proconsuls of the Roman provinces, when they drove the weaker members of the Church into blasphemy. But no such plea could be made for the men who had lived within the sound of Christ's voice, and sent Him to the Cross. In vain they had heard words such as no other man ever spake,[2] words which revealed both the Father and the Son; and their hatred for Christ proved them to be haters of God. It had been better for them if Christ had not come or had not spoken to them; for then they would have been free from the sin which a great opportunity lays to the charge of those who reject it. Nor was it the words of Christ

[1] Lc. xxiii. 34; cf. 1 Cor. ii. 8.   [2] vii. 46.

alone which the Jewish rulers of our Lord's time had refused; to His words there had been added the evidence of His works. *If I had not done among them the works that no other man did, they would not have had sin; but now have they both seen and hated both me and my Father* (xv. 24). The works of Christ, as well as His words, were without parallel in the history of Israel. Neither Moses nor Elijah nor Elisha had a record such as that of the three years' ministry of Jesus. Not only were certain of the Gospel miracles without example, such as the opening of the eyes of the man who was born blind,[1] and the walking on the sea; but no prophet had ever worked signs and wonders on so great a scale.

It is important to notice the witness which is borne more than once in the Gospel of St John to the reality and greatness of His miracles. Jesus elsewhere rebukes the spirit which sought signs and wonders, and would not believe unless they were given.[2] Many of His works were purposely done in private, and the beneficiaries were charged not to make Him known.[3] The greatest signs were wholly subsidiary to the teaching, and were illustrations of it rather than demonstrations of its truth.

---

[1] ix. 35.  [2] Mt. xii. 39, xvi. 4, Jo. iv. 48.

[3] See *e.g.* Mc. i. 43 f., where the action is accompanied by remarkable sternness: ἐμβριμησάμενος αὐτῷ εὐθὺς ἐξέβαλεν αὐτόν, καὶ λέγει αὐτῷ "Ορα μηδενὶ μηδὲν εἴπῃς.

But the historical truth of the miracles is not affected by these considerations, and it is clearly assumed in the words here attributed to our Lord.

To the Jews of Christ's time miracles offered no ntellectual difficulty. They looked for a miracle-working Messiah; yet when He came, and wrought the very miracles anticipated by the Prophets, they refused this evidence. The appeal to the eye was in this case as useless as the appeal to the ear. They had both heard and seen the Son revealed both by word and deed; they had heard and seen not the Son only, but the Father revealed in Him, and what they saw and heard had filled them with furious hatred. Some months before this they had taken up stones to cast at Jesus, and He had expostulated: "Many fair and goodly works have I shewn you from the Father; for what sort of work among these do ye stone me?"[1] The irritation then displayed had now settled into a deep, lasting hatred which was about to bear fruit in the Cross. That this would be the issue of the Lord's life of sinless service might have been expected by students of the Jewish Scriptures:

*But* so it is,[2] *that the saying may be fulfilled which is written in their Law, They hated me without cause* (xv. 25). The Jews' own sacred books had fore-

[1] x. 32.
[2] For the ellipse in ἀλλ' ἵνα cf. ix. 3, xiii. 18, xiv. 31, 1 Jo. ii. 19.

shadowed the course which the nation would take when the Christ came. The experience of the persecuted Psalmist[1] repeated itself in the experience of Messiah; He, too, was met by unmerited hostility. Gratuitous,[2] undeserved, unreasoning hatred is the natural attitude of evil towards good, and it reached its climax in the conduct of the generation which crucified Jesus. His Jewish enemies were condemned out of their own Law, which they verified by their hatred for the Christ.

Was the spell of the world's aversion never to be broken? Was Jesus not to be vindicated before the generation that condemned Him? The Lord answers this question in the last two verses of this chapter. *When the Paraclete shall come whom I will send to you from the Father, the Spirit of Truth which proceedeth from the Father, he shall bear witness concerning me; yea, and ye also shall bear witness, because ye are with me from the beginning* (xv. 26 f.).

The Incarnate will not leave Himself without witness in the world. The testimony of His words and works, which the world has rejected, will after His departure be carried forward by other witnesses. First and chief among these will be the coming Paraclete, who, as the Spirit of the Truth, cannot but

[1] Ps. xxxv. 19, lxix. 4 (LXX). The Psalms are cited as belonging to the 'Law' also in x. 34, xii. 34.

[2] The LXX rendering δωρεάν, which occurs in both Psalms, well represents the Heb. חִנָּם 'gratuitously.'

bear witness to the Truth. Hitherto the Lord has spoken of the other Paraclete only as the Teacher of the Church; He cannot teach the world while it continues to be such, for the world is not susceptible of spiritual teaching. But the Spirit may bear witness where He cannot teach as yet; and this He will do. The world had succeeded in silencing the voice of Jesus, and another generation might easily forget His teaching. But the Witness who was coming would not let the world forget, and no opposition could altogether silence Him.

'Witness' is one of the key-words of the Fourth Gospel. It is used of the preaching of John the Baptist, of our Lord's own preaching, of the testimony borne to Him by the Father at the Baptism and Transfiguration, and by His mighty works.[1] Henceforth the great witness would be the spiritual Power whose coming would follow His departure. He would take over the work of witnessing to Christ as soon as He came, and continue it to the end of time.

"The Spirit," St John says elsewhere, "it is that witnesseth";[2] that is its function in the world. Its witness is borne in the consciences of men, in the canon of Scripture, but especially in the Visible Church, through her teaching, her sacraments, her

---

[1] i. 7 f., 15, 32, 34; iii. 11, 32, v. 31 ff., viii. 13 ff. x. 25.
[2] 1 Jo. v. 6.

life, her very presence in the world as a great permanent institution that cannot be ignored, that everywhere compels attention to the Person and mission and claims of Jesus Christ.

In this world-long witness of the Spirit it was given to the Eleven to participate. "Yea, and ye also bear witness." The Divine and the human co-operate; as the Spirit bears witness with our spirits[1] in the inner life of grace, so He admits the disciples of Christ to share with Him the great work of bearing witness to the world. Our Lord Himself, before He left the world, set before the Apostles the plan of the campaign which the Spirit would enable them to accomplish; "Ye shall receive power when the Holy Spirit has come upon you, and ye shall be my witnesses both in Jerusalem, and in all Judaea and Samaria, and to the ends of the earth."[2] It belonged to the Eleven to begin this great mission, because they had been with Christ from the beginning; their companionship with Him extended over the whole of the ministry, from the Baptism to the Passion; they saw Him risen, they saw Him ascend. They were thus in a position to speak as eyewitnesses[3] of all the facts connected with the history of the Incarnate life, from the day when the Lord's public work began until the day when He passed out of the sight of men.

[1] Rom. viii. 16 τὸ πνεῦμα συνμαρτυρεῖ τῷ πνεύματι ἡμῶν.
[2] Acts i. 8.   [3] οἱ ἀπ' ἀρχῆς αὐτόπται (Lc. i. 2.)

The Eleven bore witness to their own generation, and their witness was unique as the testimony of men who had been with Jesus from the first and continued with Him to the end. But in some sense the responsibility of witnessing to Christ extends to believers in all the generations of the Church. The last eyewitness to the facts of the Gospel history must have passed away with the first century or in the early years of the second. But the witness of Christian experience remains, and the Lord expects all His disciples to take their part in it. "Ye also bear witness" is a Divine call which is heard in all ages and has reached our own time and ourselves.

## VI.

*These things have I spoken to you* (the Lord proceeds) *that ye may not be made to stumble. They will expel you from the synagogue; nay, the hour is coming that any one who killeth you will think that he offereth service to God* (xvi. 1 f).[1]

Persecution might well cause even loyal disciples to stumble, if not to fall. 'Stumbling,' a frequent metaphor in St Mark and St Matthew, is comparatively rare in the fourth Gospel;[2] it belongs more especially to the surroundings of the ministry in Galilee, where the stony ground[3] might often cause the unwary traveller to take a false step. Moral and spiritual stones of stumbling lie thick on

[1] This chapter does not, like chapter xv., begin a new section of the Discourse. It carries on and amplifies subjects already treated in part by chapters xiv., xv.: the prospect of persecution (xvi. 1-4), the sorrow caused by the Lord's departure (5 f., 16 ff., 33), the work of the Paraclete (7-15), the hope of the future (7, 16, 19 ff.), the office of prayer (23 f.), the assurance of peace and victory (32 f.).

[2] σκάνδαλον, σκανδαλίζω occurs eight times in St Mark, nineteen in St Matthew, but thrice only in St Luke and twice in St John (vi. 61, xvi. 1): see Abbott, *Voc.* 1694.

[3] Mc. iv. 16 τὰ πετρώδη: cf. 1 Pet. ii. 8 πέτρα σκανδάλου (but from Isa. viii. 14).

the way of the Church through the world, and among these the hostility of the world would be the first and most dangerous. It might well seem "a strange thing"[1] that the Lord, Himself triumphant and at rest, should suffer shame and reproach, loss of goods, and death itself to overtake His servants in the discharge of their duty to Him. They are therefore warned beforehand what they have to expect from the world after He has gone. Excommunication would be the first weapon used against the Church. Even in the lifetime of Jesus, the Jews of Jerusalem, it appears, "had agreed already that if any man should confess Him to be Christ, he should be put out of the synagogue,"[2] and the threat had deterred many from discipleship.[3] The punishment was the most serious that the spiritual power in Judaea could inflict, and for a Jew it was more formidable than exclusion from the Sacraments would seem to many Christians. The synagogue was not merely a place of religious assembly, but the centre of the life of the local Jewish community; and the excommunicated Jew was cut off not only from the ordinances of his religion, but from the society of his people, and practically reduced to the position of a Gentile.

[1] Cf. 1 Pet. iv. 12 μὴ ξενίζεσθε . . . ὡς ξένου ὑμῖν συμβαίνοντος.

[2] ix. 22, xii. 42. The word ἀποσυνάγωγος is peculiar to the fourth Gospel, but the punishment is alluded to in Lc. vi. 22. (ὅταν ἀφορίσωσιν ὑμᾶς).

[3] xii. 42.

## ST JOHN XVI. 1, 2

The sentence was pronounced in the synagogue, with the blowing of trumpets, and it seems to have been accompanied by a solemn anathema.[1] To the Eleven, who were devout Jews, and with their Master had attended the synagogues of Galilee every Sabbath day, the fear of this ignominious expulsion opened a prospect which they could not contemplate without the greatest disquietude.

But their Jewish persecutors would not stop at the infliction of social death; they would soon come to regard the actual killing of a Christian in the light of a religious service. Such was, no doubt, the point of view from which Saul looked at the stoning of Stephen, and his own subsequent attack on believers generally;[2] and the same explanation is probably to be given of the fierce hostility of the Jews towards Saul himself when he became a follower of Jesus Christ.[3] The motive was a religious one, and of the sincerity of those who were animated by it there could be no question; they had "a zeal for God, though not according to knowledge."[4] Sincerity, however, is not all that is necessary to make a religious act acceptable; murders have been committed times beyond number out of a sincere desire to do service

---

[1] See Schürer, *Jewish People* (English trans.) II. ii. p. 60 ff., with the references he gives (p. 61 f.).

[2] Cf. Acts xxvi. 9 ἔδοξα ἐμαυτῷ . . . δεῖν πολλὰ ἐναντία πρᾶξαι.

[3] Acts ix. 23, 29, xxi. 31, xxii. 22, xxiii. 12.

[4] Rom. x. 2.

to God. So it would be in the case of the Jewish adversaries of the new faith; their sincerity would add to the fury of the assault, but could not excuse it.

The root of this religious bitterness was ignorance. *And these things they will do, because they knew not the Father nor me* (xvi. 3). The Lord, as is His manner in this discourse, repeats an earlier saying, and in repeating, expands it. "They will do these things" (He had said) "because they know not Him that sent me."[1] Here He adds "nor me." Not even the human Christ, who had lived among them, was really known by the generation to which He ministered; the meaning of His mission, of His works and words, of His life and person, escaped them altogether. It was not intellectual incapacity, but a lack of apprehension arising out of spiritual blindness that prevented them from recognizing the true character of Jesus; and the same blindness explained their conduct towards the Church which represented Him when He was gone.

*But* (he continues) *these things have I spoken to you, that when the hour for them has come, ye may remember that I told you* (xvi. 4 *a*). When excommunication, imprisonment, and martyrdom overtake

---

[1] xv. 21. For οὐκ οἴδασιν τὸν πέμψαντά με we now have οὐκ ἔγνωσαν τὸν πατέρα οὐδὲ ἐμέ. Their ignorance was not absolute, but a lack of power to recognize the Divine Sonship of the Lord. Cf. Acts iii. 17 κατ' ἄγνοιαν ἐπράξατε.

you, the words I have just spoken will come back to your memory, and you will not be taken by surprise; your very sufferings will confirm your faith in me, since they have come to pass as I foretold. If the thought comes to you, Why were we not told this at the outset? the answer is ready, *These things I told you not from the beginning, because I was with you* (xvi. 4 *b*). Even in the early days of their discipleship the Lord had not concealed from His disciples that which lay before them;[1] but only towards the end had He gone into the details, for so long as He was with them there was no necessity for insisting on so alarming a prospect. But it was otherwise now: the time had come for looking the situation in the face, and preparing themselves for the rough ways of the world that lay before them.

So the Lord is brought back to His own approaching departure and the coming of the other Paraclete.

*But now I go to him that sent me, and not one of you asketh me, Where goest thou? but because I have spoken these things to you, grief hath filled your heart* (xvi. 5 f.).

" I go "[2] is the keynote of the discourse; yet often as it has been struck, no disciple has questioned the Lord about His destination. The repeated announcement has filled all with the pain of a threatened loss,

---
[1] See *e.g.* Mc. viii. 34, Mt. x. 16 ff., Lc. vi. 22.
[2] ὑπάγω: see note on xiii. 33.

but it has not roused interest or even curiosity. Simon Peter had indeed raised the question, "Where goest thou?" and Thomas had interrupted the Lord's, "Ye know the way," with the hopeless cry, "We know not where thou goest, and how know we the way?"[1] But no one had pressed the point; no eager desire had been manifested to learn the truth about it. The direction and the issue of the journey had excited no enthusiasm among the Eleven; their hearts were too full of the sense of their own bereavement. And yet the Lord's journey was closely bound up with their highest interests.

*Yet I tell you the truth; it is profitable for you that I should go away. For if I go not away, the Paraclete will assuredly not come to you; but if I take my journey, I will send him to you* (xvi. 7).

Incredible as it might seem, it was true that the disciples would gain by their loss, for it was the one condition upon which they could receive the Holy Spirit; only if Jesus left them could the other Paraclete come. There is a double mystery here. (1) We ask ourselves first why the coming of the Spirit should have depended on the going of the Son. The most obvious answer is that the Father's promised gift must be claimed by the Son's return to the Father; it was the outcome of our Lord's completed mission. In the words of St John, there could be "no

[1] xiii. 36, xiv. 5.

Spirit," that is, no effusion of the Spirit, until Jesus was glorified;[1] the Incarnate must appear in the presence of God for man, with the tokens of His accepted sacrifice, before He could send upon the Church the first-fruits of His Passion.[2] But, beyond this, it would seem that the visible Presence in the flesh and the invisible spiritual Presence could not be concurrent. The one was limited by the conditions of space and time, the other is universal; and the spiritual and universal could begin only when the visible and restricted had come to an end. (2) There remains a further question. Why was the ministry of the Spirit to be more profitable to the Church than the personal ministry of the Lord? That it could be so must have been at the time inconceivable to the Eleven; and our Lord's emphatic answer, "I tell you the truth," was necessary to silence their doubts. Yet the event has shewn that the balance of gain was greatly in favour of the post-Pentecostal Church. The Church has gained and has not lost by the Ascension;[3] in exchange for a Paraclete whose Ministry was limited to a small circle in a single

---

[1] vii. 39 οὔπω γὰρ ἦν πνεῦμα, ὅτι Ἰησοῦς οὔπω ἐδοξάσθη.

[2] Lc. xxiv. 49, Acts ii. 33.

[3] Thus Bishop Andrewes, preaching on the Ascension, paraphrases: "You conceive of my stay as beneficial to you, but falsely . . . Seeing, then, ye shall be losers by my stay and gainers by my going, be not for my stay. My stay will deprive you of Him—*non veniet* . . . my absence will procure you Him—*mittam*."

generation it has received another who can be with all believers everywhere and to the end of time. Nor in gaining the presence of the Spirit has it lost the presence of Christ, who comes wherever His Spirit comes,[1] and through the Spirit lives and works in us, and is one with us, and makes us one with Himself in the unity of the spiritual life.

Even the world which cannot receive the Spirit will benefit by His coming. *And when he has come, he will convict the world in respect of sin and of righteousness and of judgement* (xvi. 8).

There is no English word that covers the meaning of the verb used by St John.[2] Wycliffe's 'reprove,' which was followed by the Authorized Version, conveys to the modern ear little more than 'rebuke'; of the other available words neither 'convict' nor 'convince' is wholly satisfactory; 'convict' savours too much of legal formalities, 'convince' suggests a merely intellectual process. Men may be convinced by an appeal to the understanding, yet not in their consciences convicted; or *vice versa*, they may be convicted and yet not convinced. The Holy Spirit both convinces and convicts, gaining the assent of the understanding and also bringing home the charge of sin to the heart. He will at once convince and

[1] Aug. *tract.* xciv.: "neque enim ubi ille erat, iste inde recesserat." Christ, he adds, "[non] sic abscessit ut pro illo, non cum illo in eis esset Spiritus Sanctus."

[2] ἐλέγξει.

convict the world of sin, forcing men both to admit the reasonableness of the charge, and to plead guilty to it. "Which of you," our Lord had said to the Jewish world, "convicteth me of sin?"[1] But what the world could not do in His case, His Spirit will do in the case of the world, driving home upon its conscience the sense of sin which the world was not able to fasten upon Christ. In the other instances the emphasis lies on the Spirit's appeal to the intellect rather than to the moral sense, and 'convince' is nearer to the sense of the verb than 'convict.' The Paraclete will offer to the world convincing proof of the existence of Righteousness as well as of Sin, and also of the certainty of Judgement[2]—the sifting, separating process, by which sin and righteousness are distinguished and will be finally parted and assigned their rewards, and the long controversy between good and evil thus brought to an end.

The Spirit of Christ, then, will compel the world to turn its attention to these three great crucial facts which hitherto it has ignored or forgotten. It will bring men face to face with Sin, Righteousness, Judgement — not as abstractions, but in concrete realities. These the Lord proceeds to enumerate.

---

[1] viii. 46 τίς ἐξ ὑμῶν ἐλέγχει με περὶ ἁμαρτίας; The recurrence of the identical phrase ἐλέγχειν περὶ ἁμαρτίας is interesting and scarcely fortuitous.

[2] περὶ κρίσεως: cf. xii. 31.

*In respect of Sin, because they believe not on me* (xvi. 9).[1] When the rejection of the Messiah by His own nation was seen in the light of the Spirit of truth, it would be recognized as sin, and as the crowning sin of the Jewish people. The sin would be found to lie not in the mere act of crucifying Jesus, but in the unbelief which lay at the root of their whole attitude towards Him. Nothing seemed more unlikely than that any number of those who had refused to believe while the Lord was among them should after His departure be stricken with remorse, when the sin was laid to their charge by one of His disciples. Yet this moral miracle was wrought, if we believe the witness of St Luke; St Peter's audience on the day of Pentecost were "pricked in their hearts," and cried "What shall we do?"[2]—convinced, not by the force of St Peter's eloquence, but by the invisible power of the Spirit of conviction. The miracle is repeated to-day, when men who have hitherto thought of faith in Christ as an intellectual bondage, against which the finer spirits rightly rebel, are brought to see that unbelief is not only a sin but the chief of sins. Such things happen; and when they do, we

---

[1] On ὅτι (verses 9-11) see Abbott, *Gr.* 2178-2182. There is perhaps a subtle difference in the use of the conjunction in each case: ὅτι οὐ πιστεύουσιν, "in that they believe not"; ὅτι . . . ὑπάγω, "by reason of the fact that I go"; ὅτι . . . κέκριται, "forasmuch as he has been judged already."

[2] Acts ii. 37.

know that the Spirit has come who convicts the world of sin because it has not believed in the Only-begotten Son of God.

*In respect of Righteousness, again, because I go to the Father, and ye behold me no more* (xvi. 10). A life of perfect righteousness has been lived on earth, and the world knew it not, because the world's standard of righteousness was of another kind. The Jewish world thought of righteousness as the fulfilment of stated external acts, prescribed in the Torah or by the traditions of its great religious teachers; and in these acts it found Jesus wanting, and in some instances deliberately so. Sinlessness in act, word, and thought, entire devotion to the will of God, absolute self-sacrifice, other-worldliness combined with enthusiasm for humanity, constant fellowship with God, sympathetic intercourse with sinful men,—righteousness such as this did not appeal to our Lord's generation. Such a life needed to be removed to another sphere before it could be seen to be what it was; only the Spirit of Christ could reveal to men His true character, and He would reveal it only when the earthly life was ended, and Jesus was with the Father, unseen by the bodily eye. In its fullest measure this conviction of righteousness, this deeper sense of the glory of the perfect life, is found only in those who are led by the Spirit and endeavour to . follow the steps of the Christ-life. But the Spirit has to some extent convinced the world itself. The world has come by common consent to recognize in Jesus Christ the highest example of goodness. It has repented of its treatment of the Holy and Righteous One; and if it does not yet agree to confess Him as the Son of God, at least it sees in Him the ideal Son of Man. And this conviction has profoundly changed human life, raising the standard of moral conduct even in a society which is not professedly Christian. Through the Gospels and the Church the Spirit has impressed the world with an ideal of righteousness, which, it may be hoped, will not be wholly lost again.

*In respect of Judgement, once more, because the Ruler of the world hath been judged* (xvi. 11).

"Now is the judgement of this world," the Lord had said a little while before; "now shall the Ruler of this world be cast out";[1] and this evening, at the end of the first section of the Discourse, He had added, "The Ruler of the world cometh, and in me he hath not anything."[2] But now He speaks as if all were accomplished. The world's Ruler had been judged; sentence had been passed on him already; he had been weighed in the balances, and found wanting. To-morrow would proclaim the victory which had already been won in the field of the will. The righteous life of Jesus, unsullied to the end by

[1] xii. 31.      [2] xiv. 30.

a single sin, was itself the judgement of the Evil One; henceforth he would be a beaten and discredited enemy. The casting out of Satan might not be yet, for the unclean spirit in man is not easily exorcized; two generations after the Passion St John still sadly confesses that "the whole world lieth in the Evil One."[1] But sentence had been pronounced on him already by the fact of Christ's triumph. The world itself witnesses to this in its own way. No reader of history who compares ancient with modern life, the abominations that defaced Greek and Roman civilization with the lighter evils which afflict society since it has been baptized into Christ, will fail to realize the truth of Christ's verdict on Satan. The saying lately recovered from a MS. of the appendix to St Mark, whether a genuine reminiscence or not, is surely true: "the limit of the years of Satan's rule has been reached and passed";[2] it was passed when Jesus Christ died and rose again. And the world itself has in its own way grasped the reality of the death-blow dealt to the power of Evil by the Cross.

With the coming of the Spirit there would come— there has come, as we may now add—a new era of moral judgements. The Gospel has brought to

[1] 1 Jo. v. 19.

[2] πεπλήρωται ὁ ὅρος τῶν ἐτῶν τῆς ἐξουσίας τοῦ σατανᾶ. It is added, ἀλλὰ ἐγγίζει ἄλλα δεινὰ καὶ ὑπὲρ ὧν ἐγὼ ἁμαρτησάντων παρεδόθην. The saying is reported in part by Jerome in a Latin version; the Greek text came to light in 1906.

mankind a new conception of sin, a new standard of righteousness, a new realization of the impending doom of the one and victory of the other. The death and resurrection of Jesus have changed all; and the Spirit has impressed this change upon the conscience of humanity. The new heaven and the new earth will follow in due time, when the age-long work of the Spirit is ended.

## VII.

FROM the work of the Paraclete in the world the Lord passes to His work in the Church. Here the Spirit of Christ will carry forward and complete Christ's preparatory teaching.

*I have yet many things to say to you, but ye cannot bear them now* (xvi. 12).

The teaching of the Ministry was in one sense complete in itself; all that is fundamental in Christian thought and life found a place in it. Nevertheless, much yet remained to be said which could not be said at the time, not through want of power on the part of the Teacher to say it, but because it was then beyond the capacity of His followers. A wise teacher does not attempt to teach children the advanced lessons which are the food of adults. Such teaching as the Church afterwards received from St Paul[1] and St John, and in yet later days from an Athanasius, a Basil, an Augustine, would have been an intolerable load upon the immature powers of the Twelve in the days of their

[1] St Paul himself was well aware of the need of reserve with younger or weaker converts; see 1 Cor. iii. 1 f. Cf. Heb. v. 12 ff., 1 Peter ii. 2.

discipleship. They were still in the childhood of their spiritual growth; the burden[1] of a larger teaching would have taxed their strength too heavily. The wise and tender care of the Great Master to lay upon His disciples no more than they could assimilate explains the simplicity of His manner, and the form in which many of His profoundest sayings are cast. He was addressing Himself to the intelligence of beginners in the spiritual life; the sayings and discourses of the Ministry were not to be His final utterances; He would teach them more hereafter by His Spirit.

*But when He has come, the Spirit of Truth, He shall guide you into the whole truth, for He shall not speak from Himself, but shall speak whatsoever He heareth, and shall announce to you the things that are coming* (xvi. 13).

'What you could not learn from me while I was with you, the other Paraclete will gradually impart when I am gone. He is the Spirit of Truth, of the Truth itself;[2] and it is therefore His province to guide you into the ways of truth, and of the whole truth.' For the office of the Spirit in the Church is to guide and lead, not to compel; and to teach by suggestion, rather than in a dogmatic and final form.

---

[1] οὐ δύνασθε βαστάζειν. For this sense of βαστάζειν see Acts xv. 10, Gal. vi. 2, 5.

[2] τῆς ἀληθείας: cf. xiv. 6, 17, xv. 26, xvi. 13.

The Lord uses a word[1] which frequently occurs in the Greek Old Testament in connexion with God's dealings with Israel. God, we read, 'led' Israel from Egypt by the pillar of cloud by day and by fire by night.[2] In the Psalms the same word is used in reference to the guidance of the individual life; "lead me in Thy righteousness," "lead me in Thy truth"; "lead me in the way everlasting"; "let thy good spirit lead me in the right path"; "he leadeth me in the paths of righteousness"; "the meek will he lead in judgment"—all these and other passages assume the presence in human life of a Divine Guide.[3] In our Lord's last discourse the Guide is revealed. The other Paraclete is to be our Guide, as the Lord Himself is our Way.[4]

The Spirit guides into the Truth, and the Truth into which He guides is the whole and not a part. God, who spoke to the fathers in the prophets by divers portions, speaks to us through the Spirit of His Son fully and finally. So long as we are in this world there is no other guidance to follow the guidance of the Spirit, nor any more complete revelation to take the place of that which He makes to the Church and to the soul. But though the truth into

---

[1] ὁδηγήσει: cf. the use of ὁδηγεῖν in Mt. xv. 14, Acts viii. 31, Apoc. vii. 17.

[2] Num. xxiv. 8, Deut. i. 33.

[3] Ps. v. 8, xxv. 5, 9, xxxi. 3, cxxxviii. 24, cxlii. 10 (LXX).

[4] The ὁδός which the ὁδηγός reveals.

which He leads is complete, the leading is gradual, and always, while we are here, falls short of the end; otherwise He would cease to lead. The Lord's words therefore contain no promise of infallibility or of full attainment, either for the living Church in any age or for any individual Christian, whatever may be his position in the Church. Nor does the promise of the Spirit's guidance secure to any individual even a partial attainment of truth, except on the condition of following the Guide. Thus full scope is left for human effort, and for the sense of responsibility; while no absolute security is given against human infirmity and error. The Lord guarantees only that the Spirit who cannot err, who is the very Spirit of truth, shall not cease to guide the Church until all truth has been reached. Here, as elsewhere in this discourse, the Eleven are primarily in view; but the promise is not to be restricted to the Eleven, or to the first generation, or the first few centuries. It is the permanent function of the Spirit to lead, and the first necessity for the Church to follow His guidance, to the end of time.

The Lord adds that the Spirit will teach nothing but that which He has Himself received from the ultimate Source of truth. As the Son, in His earthly life, could do nothing and say nothing from Himself, but only that which He had seen the Father do and had heard from the Father,[1] so the Spirit is not an independent source of teaching; the truth into which He guides is not of His own creation or discovery; the enlarged views, the more exact apprehension, the new presentations of truth which the Church will receive from the Spirit, have been received by the Spirit from the Father. The only difference herein between the Son and the Spirit is that in the order of the Divine life the Son receives immediately, and the Spirit mediately, through the Son.[2] The Spirit is ever receiving,[3] and ever imparting what He receives: not a new revelation, but new interpretations of the original message. "He will tell you,"[4] the Lord adds, "things that are to come." "When the Christ comes He will tell us all things," was the simple creed of the Samaritan woman.[5] The Christ had come and was about to go; yet much remained to be told; and He passes on this Messianic function to the other Paraclete who is to carry on His work.

[1] Cf. v. 30, vii. 17, viii. 26, xii. 49, xiv. 10.

[2] Thus Gregory of Nyssa speaks, *Quod non sint tres dii*, 133: the Son is τὸ προσεχῶς ἐκ τοῦ πρώτου, the Spirit τὸ διὰ τοῦ προσεχῶς ἐκ τοῦ πρώτου: cf. *The Holy Spirit in the ancient Church*, p. 252. The order of 'receiving' follows the order of life.

[3] Westcott points out that the Son taught ὃ ἤκουσεν, but the Spirit teaches ὅσα ἀκούει. The message of the Spirit is continuous to the end of time.

[4] ἀναγγελεῖ. The verb is used of 'reporting' facts, and especially of the preaching of the Gospel (Acts xx. 20, 27, 1 Pet. i. 12, 1 Jo. i. 5).

[5] iv. 25 ὅταν ἔλθῃ ἐκεῖνος ἀναγγελεῖ ἡμῖν ἅπαντα.

The Spirit is to declare to the Church, that the Church may declare to the world, "the things that are to come,"[1] *i.e.* the new order, the dispensation which is to begin at Pentecost. It is not prediction only or chiefly that is here attributed to the Spirit, but rather the unfolding, in the consciousness of the Church, of the whole mystery of Christ—the doctrine, the Sacraments, the life of the Body of Christ. All this to the Eleven was as yet hidden and future, but would hereafter be revealed and verified in their own experience, and in the experience of the Christian centuries. The Lord proceeds:

*He—the Paraclete—shall glorify me, in that he shall take of that which is mine and declare it to you. All things whatsoever the Father hath are mine; for this reason I said that he taketh of that which is mine, and shall declare it to you* (xvi. 14 f.).

To declare the glories of the coming dispensation will be in effect to glorify Jesus, who is its Author. The Spirit will glorify the Son, as the Son glorified the Father, by revealing His glory. The Spirit will do this, not by imparting to Him new attributes, nor by clothing Him, in the imagination of the Church, with a new character; but simply by shewing Him to His disciples as He was and is, in the light of His own inherent wealth of Divine perfections. In

---

[1] τὰ ἐρχόμενα: cf. Heb. ii. 5 τὴν οἰκουμένην τὴν μέλλουσαν, *i.e.* the new dispensation.

the new dispensation Christ is "all things"[1]; but the glorification of Jesus is a progressive work, of which the steps may be noted in the history and writings of the Apostolic age, as the Spirit takes more and more of that which is Christ's and shews it to the teachers of the Church. No one can read the Epistles of St Paul or the Gospel of St John without having before him evidence that this part of our Lord's promise concerning the work of the Paraclete was fulfilled to the first generation. All serious students of the New Testament are conscious of a profound difference between the historical Jesus of the Synoptic Gospels and the Christ of the Epistles, the Incarnate Word of the Fourth Gospel. To the plain man who believes that our Lord spoke some such words as those now under consideration, the difference presents no ultimate difficulty; he sees in the Synoptic Jesus a portrait of Christ as He manifested Himself in the days of the flesh, and in the conceptions of St Paul and St John the same Person transfigured by the Spirit's revelation of the glory of the Incarnate Son.

There is at the present time a disposition to regard the later picture as exaggerated by the haze which the lapse of time threw around the primitive figure of the Lord. We are asked to content

[1] Col. iii. 11 πάντα καὶ ἐν πᾶσιν Χριστός.

ourselves with the original conception as it appears in the first three Gospels, or rather with that which is left of it when the Gospels have been denuded of all that recent criticism counts untrustworthy. But to do so is to limit ourselves to a partial view of truth, when the whole is within our reach: to ignore the work of the other Paraclete, to whom it belonged to glorify Jesus by revealing that which is His in the later experience of the Apostolic age.

Exaggeration is hardly possible here, if, as the Lord proceeds to say, all things whatsoever the Father has are His. In the belief of the ancient Church, which is based on that of the first age, there is nothing that the two Persons have not in common, except the personal distinction of Father and Son: nothing that belongs to the Father, beyond the Fatherhood, which does not belong to the Son. But this belief does not exceed the tenor of Christ's own words here; and His words here are in substance repeated in the Last Prayer when He looks up to heaven and says in the Face of God: "The things that are mine are all thine, and the things that are thine are mine."[1] The riches of Christ are, in St Paul's phrase, "unsearchable,"[2] because they

[1] xvii. 10.

[2] Eph. iii. 8 τὸ ἀνεξιχνίαστον πλοῦτος τοῦ χριστοῦ. The adjective is used in one other passage only (Rom. xi. 33), and then of the ways of God, and with the same sense of unspeakable wealth (ὦ βάθος πλούτου); cf. Job v. 9, ix. 10, xxxiv. 24 (LXX).

are the riches of God; there is in Him, as St Paul knew, all that is necessary for the satisfaction of the intellect and the spirit of man, because there is in Him all that is in God, the whole content of the Divine Essence. All this the Spirit which proceeds from the Father, and is the Spirit of the Son, takes [1] —the present tense covers the whole world-long process—and will declare to men—in Scripture, in the creeds and preaching of the Church, in the witness of the saints, in the experience of life, in the thoughts and words of great Christian teachers, in the unspoken, half conscious testimony of the simplest believers.

Thus the departure of the visible Jesus from the world was in no way to deprive the disciples of their conscious realization of Himself, but on the contrary it would intensify their sense of His fulness.

[1] λαμβάνει takes the place of λήμψεται (v. 14), though ἀναγγελεῖ remains. Historically the age-long process will work itself out in future details beyond the present comprehension of the Eleven.

## VIII.

*A little while, and ye behold*[1] *me no more; and again a little while, and ye shall see*[1] *me* (xvi. 16).

In a few hours, if we date His departure from His death, or if from His Ascension in a few weeks, He would be hidden from the sight of their eyes. At the Ascension they gazed up after Him, but in vain; a cloud received Him out of their sight, and they beheld Him no more. The spiritual cannot be apprehended by the fleshly sight, but only by spiritual vision. But the latter began when the former ended; the Ascension, followed by the coming of the Spirit, opened the eyes of the understanding and of the heart to see the Lord as He had never been seen before.

To the Eleven, who still realized little of what the future held for them, this last saying was enig-

---

[1] θεωρεῖτε is used of the bodily eyesight, while ὄψεσθε refers to the spiritual vision which the coming of the Spirit would bring. In xiv. 10 θεωρεῖν is used of both modes of apprehension; in xvi. 10, and here, of the former only. Strictly speaking, θεωρεῖν is to be spectator of some sight which appeals to the eye (cf. Jo. ii. 23, vi. 3, Lc. xxiv. 37); ὁρᾶν may refer to a purely spiritual object (*e.g.* Mt. v. 8 τὸν θεὸν ὄψονται (Heb. xi. 27 τὸν ἀόρατον ὡς ὁρῶν).

matical. It seemed to present a contradiction in terms: "Ye shall not behold ... ye shall see"; and one whispered to another, seeking an explanation. *Some of his disciples therefore said one to the other, What is this that he saith to us, A little while, and ye behold me not, and again a little while and ye shall see me? And, Because I go to the Father? They said therefore, What is this that he calleth 'A little while'? We know not of what he speaketh* (xvi. 17 f.). But no light could be gained from their fellow disciples, and they feared to interrupt the Master again. The Lord, however, had understood their whisperings, and Himself answered their questions so far as an answer was possible at this stage. *Jesus knew that they wished to ask him, and said to them, Is it concerning this that ye inquire one with another, that I said, A little while, and ye behold me not, and again a little while and ye shall see me?* (xvi. 19 f.).

"Jesus knew." Our Evangelist frequently calls attention to the Lord's insight into character and fact. "He knew all men," we read; "He knew what was in man." He "knew that the Pharisees had heard"; that the crowd in Galilee were "about to make Him King." He knows His sheep—who they are that love Him.[1] The same unique knowledge appears here. He does not, it seems, overhear the words spoken, but He grasps at once what the

[1] Jo. ii. 24 f., iv. 1, vi. 15, x. 14, 27, xxi. 17.

whisperings mean ; He realizes the perplexity of the Eleven, their desire to ask Him, and their reluctance to do so, and He supplies the answer without waiting to hear the question. We need not try to determine whether this singular power of reading men's thoughts is to be ascribed to human intuition or to Divine omniscience ; perhaps a truer explanation is that His human powers were heightened by the Divine indwelling, just as, on the other side, His exercise of Divine powers was limited by the finite nature through which they operated.[1]

Jesus knew that the Eleven wished but did not dare to put to Him the questions which they had put to one another. They had asked no question of Him since the ventures of Thomas, Philip, and Judas ; they feared to expose their own ignorance and merit His reproof. The Lord had not, as it seems, encouraged the asking of questions on this occasion, perhaps because the time was all too short for that which He had to say, perhaps also because He looked to the Spirit to interpret His meaning. But here was a question which exercised them all, and it was necessary to their peace that they should receive an immediate answer so far as it could be given. His answer is for the heart rather than for the understanding :

*Verily, verily, I say to you that ye shall weep and wail, but the world shall rejoice; ye shall be*

[1] See Weston, *The One Christ*, p. 193 ff.

*grieved, but your grief shall be turned into joy* (xvi. 20).

As if He had said: 'Do not perplex yourselves about the "little while" and the other details of my saying, but simply believe my word when I tell you that a time is coming, first of bitter sorrow, and then of exultant joy, and that the transition from sorrow to joy will be speedy; the whole experience in both its stages will occupy but a brief period of time.' The pain will be so sharp as to resemble the agony of a great bereavement, and the Lord uses words which recall the loud sobbing and the wailing dirge that accompanied the burial of the dead, and the deeper grief of the widow and orphan who have lost their best friend and protector.[1] So the Eleven would mourn the dead Christ on that awful Sabbath that intervened between the Crucifixion and the Resurrection;[2] no loss of husband or father was ever more keenly felt. And all the while the Jewish world, scribe and Pharisee and elder and priest, would be

[1] κλαύσετε καὶ θρηνήσετε . . . λυπηθήσεσθε. Cf. Lc. vii. 32, where children, playing at a funeral, complain to some irresponsive fellows, ἐθρηνήσαμεν καὶ οὐκ ἐκλαύσατε, "we sang a dirge, and you did not accompany it with lamentations." λυπεῖσθαι denotes the real sorrow of the relatives (1 Thess. iv. 13).

[2] The older Gospels are remarkably reticent about the Apostles' grief; only the women who accompanied the Lord to the Cross are related to have indulged in the loud lamentations which accompany an eastern funeral (Lc. xxiii. 27 ἐκόπτοντο καὶ ἐθρήνουν αὐτόν). But see the appendix to Mc. (xvi. 20 πενθοῦσι καὶ κλαίουσιν) and the Gospel of Peter 12 ἡμεῖς οἱ δώδεκα . . . ἐκλαίομεν καὶ ἐλυπούμεθα.

rejoicing in the thought that it was rid of the Prophet who disturbed their peace. But the greater the disciples' sense of sorrow and loss, the more deep and lasting would be their joy when they saw Him again. "Then were the disciples glad when they saw the Lord"[1]—so St John writes, perhaps with reference to the present passage. The twofold experience must have repeated itself at the Ascension in a less degree; even the joy of the Lord's exaltation could not but have been dimmed at first by the sense of separation, until the Spirit came, and they saw the glorified Christ with the open eye of spiritual sight. The "joy of the Holy Ghost" is a commonplace of the Acts and Epistles.[2] Yet the New Testament holds out to believers the prospect of a greater joy when the Lord comes again; when at length "death shall be no more, neither shall there be mourning nor crying nor pain any more";[3] when He shall be seen as He is, the Risen by the risen, with the new faculties of the spiritual body.[4] Nor is this final instalment of joy so far from the Church as it may seem to be: "yet a little while, and He that cometh shall come."[5]

---

[1] xx. 20.     [2] Rom. xiv. 17; Gal. v. 22; 1 Thess. i. 6.
[3] Apoc. xxi. 4.     [4] 1 Jo. iii. 2.

[5] Heb. x. 37. Even the present joy of believing has caught the brightness of the more glorious future: see 1 Pet. i. 8 $\chi\alpha\rho\hat{q}$ ... $\delta\epsilon\delta o\xi\alpha\sigma\mu\acute{\epsilon}\nu\eta$, with Hort's note.

So the great words of Christ fulfil themselves in many ways; no one interpretation exhausts their meaning. A complete answer to the question raised by the Eleven can only be given by the whole experience of the Church; no short or simple explanation can be other than partial and incomplete.

An illustration is added of the sudden transition of which the Lord had spoken: *A woman[1] when she is in childbirth hath grief, because her hour has come; but when she has given birth to the child, she remembers her distress no longer, for her joy that a man has been born into the world* (xvi. 21). In this case it is physical anguish that issues in joy, but the principle is the same. A time comes in the mother's experience when she must suffer, but it soon passes, and the suffering is succeeded by a joy so deep as to blot out the memory of her pain. So, not long hence, the disciples will forget their sorrow.

But the illustration suggests more than this. The result of the mother's pain is to bring a new human being into the world. All the possibilities of a human life arise out of that short agony. So out of the sorrow of the bereaved Apostles there would grow the new life of the Christian Church, with its infinite potentiality for good. The coming of the

---

[1] ἡ γυνή: the generic article points to the sex represented in a particular instance.

## THE LAST DISCOURSE

Spirit was to be the new birth of the race; a new humanity was thereby born into the world, and in the joy of the new creation the Apostolic Church forgot the anguish of the days when the Lord was taken from her. Without that anguish there could have been no Easter, no Ascension Day, no Pentecost; no new birth of heaven and earth.[1] The sufferings of the Eleven were the travail-pains which ushered in the birth of the universal Church.

*Even so ye, then, now have grief; but I will see you again, and your heart shall be glad, and your joy none shall take from you* (xvi. 22).

"Ye shall see me," the Lord had said before;[2] but now He changes this into "I will see you again." He would turn their thoughts from themselves to Him; He will share in the joy of the renewed intercourse; for in His Spirit He will see them even as He shall be seen by them. As for the disciples, their joy would be lasting as well as deep; their hearts, now troubled and disposed to play the coward, would rejoice with a joy which none could take from them. All earthly things can be taken away, and so in some circumstances can things that are spiritual and in themselves enduring. "He that hath not," the Master

---

[1] Cf. Isa. lxvi. 7 ff., Hosea xiii. 13, where the same figure represents the new birth of a restored Israel. See also in the N.T. Rom. viii. 14 ff., Gal. iv. 19.

[2] xvi. 17 ὄψεσθέ με : 22 ὄψομαι ὑμᾶς.

has said, "from him shall be taken away even that which he hath"; and again, in the parable of the talents, "Take ye away the talent from him"—from the slothful servant who had hid his talent in the earth.[1] But no such final loss awaits those to whom the sight of Christ is the chief joy of life.

[1] Mc. iv. 25, Mt. xxv. 28.

## IX.

The Lord now adds something about those coming days of joy when He shall see His disciples again:

*And in that day ye shall ask me no question. Verily, verily, I say unto you, If ye shall ask the Father for aught, he shall give it you in my name* (xvi. 23).

"Ye shall ask me no question"[1] calls the thoughts of the disciples back to the question which they had feared to put, but which He had interpreted and partly answered. When He saw them again, how many questions they would have to put! how much He would have to explain! So they might think; but, as a matter of fact, all such intercourse by question and answer was at an end, and His return would not bring it back. There would be no need for it when the Spirit had come to guide them into all the truth, when the questionings which still awaited an answer would be gradually solved by the growing light of the Paraclete illuminating their own faculties and interpreting to them the teaching of Scripture and the experience of life.

[1] ἐμὲ οὐκ ἐρωτήσετε οὐδέν.

But if, in the coming age, there would be no need or desire to interrogate a visible Christ, nor any opportunity of doing so, access to the Father would be easy and fruitful in answers to prayer.[1] The promise of such access had already been made in more than one form. "Whatsoever ye shall ask the Father in my name, I will do it," or "He shall give it you"[2]—so the Lord had said hitherto; but now He changes the order, saying "Whatsoever ye shall ask the Father, He will give it you in my name." The name of Jesus Christ is both the passport by which His disciples may claim access into the audience chamber of God, and the medium through which the Divine answer comes.

All this, so familiar to ourselves, was still new to the Eleven; it was not as yet a part of their experience. *Until now ye asked nothing in my name; ask, and ye shall receive, that your joy may be fulfilled* (xvi. 24). The simpler precept and promise, "Ask, and ye shall receive," belongs to the early teaching of the Ministry;[3] but the condition "in my name" was reserved to the end, for it could not be fulfilled until the new and living way to the Father was opened by the entrance of the Lord into the Holiest, and revealed to the Church by the coming of the Spirit. Even before this, even

---

[1] ἄν τι αἰτήσητε τὸν πατέρα, where αἰτεῖν takes the place of ἐρωτᾶν.

[2] xiv. 13 f., xv. 16.   [3] Mt. vii. 7.

under the old covenant, prayer had been the great resource of all believers; but the new factor which the Lord revealed when He directed that prayer should henceforth be offered in His name gives the Church an assurance which makes approach to the Father not only our wisdom and our duty but our joy. In proportion as we use the Name in our prayers, entering the Divine Presence by the new and living Way, our joy approaches fulness,[1] up to our capacity. To realize our Lord's mediation and to draw near to the Father through Him in the Holy Spirit, is to find a spring of happiness which can never fail.[2]

*These things have I spoken to you in proverbs;*[3] *the hour is coming when I shall speak to you in proverbs no longer, but with plainness of speech*[4] *I shall tell you concerning the Father* (xvi. 25).

---

[1] With $ᾗ$ $πεπληρωμένη$ compare 1 Jo. i. 4 (with Brooke's note) and 2 Jo. 12.

[2] Rom. v. 1 f. shews that the experience of the primitive Church answered to this promise of Christ.

[3] $ἐν$ $παροιμίαις$ . . . $παρρησίᾳ$. The alliteration is probably intentional, and it is kept up in the Latin version ("non in proverbiis sed palam") as well as in our own A.V. and R.V. ("no more in proverbs but . . . plainly").

[4] $παροιμίαι$ is the LXX rendering of מְשָׁלִים in the title of Proverbs, *i.e.* it represents the terse sententious sayings which make up the greater part of that book. But such sayings often rest on some similitude, and מָשָׁל is accordingly rendered in Ezek. xvii. 2 and other similar contexts by $παραβολή$. Nearly in the latter sense it is used by St John

The Lord reviews His past teaching and compares it with His teaching in the future—in the days when sorrow shall have been turned into joy. So far all His teaching had been expressed in proverbs; henceforth all would be in plain words. "In proverbs" is an inadequate rendering, but the English language supplies no exact equivalent.[1] The words cover the *logia*, the short sententious sayings of the Ministry, as well as the whole of our Lord's parabolic teaching. All He had taught had been conveyed hitherto in symbols rather than in direct utterance. The time for plain, open speech had not come so long as He was on earth. There were indeed occasions on which He seemed to speak quite freely and directly.[1] But though some of His sayings were relatively plain, there was always in what He said more than lay on the surface—more than could be understood by His hearers at the time. If the Lord ever spoke with perfect freedom, He would assuredly have done so on this last night when He was alone with the Eleven and the end had come; yet, as He tells them, the parabolic or 'paroemiae' form of teaching was still maintained. The simple, almost naïve, words of the Last Discourse

in x. 6; here, however, the reference is evidently wider and the παροιμίαι of Christ are not the parables only but the sayings of the Ministry in general.

[1] At Jerusalem, where His teaching seems to have been more explicit than in Galilee, it was once said of Him (vii. 26) ἴδε παρρησίᾳ λαλεῖ, as if this were unusual. See also Mc. viii. 31, Jo. xviii. 20.

# THE LAST DISCOURSE

went far beyond the disciples' power of apprehension; that this was so is made evident by their questions, or, when they did not dare to question, by their perplexity.

But all this was to be changed. The time was at hand when proverb and parable, allegory and symbol would be done away: when words would no longer conceal but express the truth. Obscurity would then give place to luminous clearness; if the teaching of Christ in the flesh had seemed to be characterized by the former, the latter would mark His teaching in the Spirit.

In what field would this plainer, more direct teaching lie? The Lord answers that it would find a place in future revelations of the Father. He had taught His disciples much about the Father already; His own life had been a revelation of God;[1] those who saw Him had seen the Father.[2] Yet all this was proverb and parable compared with the open vision which was to follow. When the Son had returned in His perfected manhood to the Father He would report to His brethren what He found in that infinite Source of truth.[3] His Spirit, fresh from the presence of the Very Truth, would announce to the hearts of

---

[1] He had been, as was afterwards seen, the Father's Exegete (i. 18 θεὸν . . . ἐκεῖνος ἐξηγήσατο).

[2] xiv. 9.

[3] περὶ τοῦ πατρὸς ἀπαγγελῶ ὑμῖν. Cf. ἀναγγελεῖ used in verses 13, 14 of the Spirit, who will 'announce' what the Son 'reports.'

believers more than words can utter, with a plainness, a directness, a freedom of speech which Jesus Himself, when on earth, could not use.

There is no limit to the progressive accomplishment of this great promise. We can see its initial fulfilment in the experience of the Apostolic age, and of every succeeding age of the Church, including our own. It is reasonable to expect that as the world grows older the teaching of the Spirit of Christ will grow both fuller and clearer. New lights will illumine the words of Scripture and the Creeds; there will be new interpretations of God as He is to be seen in Nature, in history, in thought; and in all such accretions of knowledge believers are entitled to hear the voice of the glorified Christ reporting what He has seen and heard in the heavenly sphere with a clearness of which the first generation of Christians had no experience. But the complete revelation is not yet, nor perhaps within the present order; it awaits the day when we shall see face to face, when our Lord will tell us concerning the Father, not in human words but in the language of the Father's House.

*In that day ye shall ask in my name, and I say not to you that I will enquire of the Father concerning you; for the Father himself loveth you, because ye have loved me and have believed that I came forth from the Father* (xvi. 26 f.).

Fuller and clearer knowledge will bring more perfect access to the Father, more adequate use of the mediation of the Son. Even in that time of clearer light, access must be through the Son. But this does not imply that there is some reluctance on the part of the Father to receive prayer, which needs to be overcome by the intercession of the Son. There is no need for the Great Intercessor to enquire[1] what is the Father's attitude or will with regard to the loyal followers of Jesus Christ; the Father Himself, of His own motion, and apart from any such intervention, loves those who love and believe in His Beloved Son. And the Eleven had both loved and believed. Their love to Christ had rarely risen above earthly standards or exceeded natural affection; they had regarded Him with the love of the scholar for the master, and not with the deeper love with which He loved them.[2] Yet their love, earthly as it was, awoke an answer in the heart of God; the Father Himself reciprocated the loyalty of the men who had loved the Son in the days of His ministry, and had continued faithful to the end.[3] Their faith, again, was limited in scope; it went little further than an

[1] οὐ λέγω ὑμῖν ὅτι ἐγὼ ἐρωτήσω τὸν πατέρα περὶ ὑμῶν. Compare with this xiv. 16, xvii. 9, 20.

[2] It has been noted that in xxi. 15 Peter does not venture to take up the great challenge of the Lord's ἀγαπᾷς με (cf. xiv. 23), though he can confidently reiterate his φιλῶ σε.

[3] πεφιλήκατε καὶ πεπιστεύκατε.

acceptance of the Lord's mission. "God, of God," and the rest of the Nicene Confession, would have had no meaning for them; they believed that He came forth from God, but scarcely as yet that He was Himself God.[1] But their faith, if immature and undeveloped, was genuine and on the right lines; and like their love, it would survive the shock of the Crucifixion. Such faith, however imperfect, was sure of the Divine acceptance.

[1] The extent of their creed was παρὰ (or ἀπὸ) τοῦ πατρὸs ἐξῆλθεν (xvi. 27, 30; xviii. 8); for θεὸs ἐκ θεοῦ they were not ripe as yet.

## X.

*I came out from the Father, and am come into the world; again, I leave the world, and am going to the Father* (xvi. 28).

The Lord sets His seal to the creed of the Eleven, which, so far as it went, was true—that He came forth, or (as He prefers to say) out from the Father,[1] and came into the world, entering the sphere of created life and assuming the form of man, the servant of God. To this *credendum* let them add another: that He was now leaving the world and returning in His human form to God. These few words embrace the whole of the primitive creed—the Incarnation, the life and death, the Resurrection and Ascension of the Lord. It all seemed to the Apostles absolutely clear, putting into plain, direct words that which the Master had taught them about Himself. "I came from the Father into the world; I leave the world and go to the Father"—what could be more explicit, more free from ambiguity? Surely the time

[1] He changes παρὰ into ἐκ (xvi. 27, 28); cf. viii. 42.

for plainness of speech, which the Lord foretold, had come already.

*His disciples say, Lo, thou speakest plainly now, and it is no proverb that thou sayest; now we know that thou knowest all things, and hast no need that any ask thee questions; hereby we believe that it was from God*[1] *that thou camest forth* (xvi. 29 f.).

The doubt raised in their minds by the obscurity of the saying, "A little while,"[2] has been dispelled by the plain speaking they have just heard. It had set them free from the suspicion that Jesus did not Himself know what He was saying; that He needed to have His thoughts cleared by interrogation. Without any questioning on their part He had made His meaning clear, He had had His answer ready; and He could in like manner resolve all their doubts. He knew everything; and this perfect knowledge, this readiness to clear up all difficulties, proclaimed Him to be in truth, as they believed, from God. It was a belated and an inadequate confession of their faith, coming, as it did, from the Lord's immediate followers and at the end of a long discipleship; and the Lord's answer shews His dissatisfaction.

*Jesus answered them, Is it only now that ye believe? Behold, an hour cometh, yea, is come, that ye be scattered*

---

[1] ἀπὸ θεοῦ falls short of the Lord's ἐκ θεοῦ (v. 28), and even of παρὰ τοῦ πατρὸς (v. 27): cf. Lc. i. 26 (yet see Jo. i. 6).

[2] They had exclaimed: οὐκ οἴδαμεν τί λέγει (xvi. 18).

*each to his own quarters, and leave me alone ; and yet
I am not alone, because the Father is with me* (xvi. 31 f.).

"Now" in Christ's answer is more emphatic than in the disciples' utterance.[1] 'Is this the moment you have chosen to profess belief in me? Have you left this primary duty to the eve of the Passion? Will so late, not to say so incomplete, a faith support you in the crisis that is imminent?' Then He flashes across the near future a searchlight which reveals the danger of the next twelve hours. 'An hour is coming, indeed it has come already,[2] when every one of you will desert your Master. Like sheep scattered by the wolf,[3] you will flee hither and thither intent on reaching your several shelters, and regardless of the safety of the Shepherd.' The disgraceful scene which verified this prediction is related by the Synoptists with a fidelity which inspires confidence in their trustworthiness. Each disciple, it seems, upon the arrest of the Master, fled to his own lodging,[4] and remained there till, the immediate danger ended by the crucifixion and death of Jesus, they began again to gather in the upper room of the Last Supper.

[1] They had said: $ν \hat{υ} ν$ οἴδαμεν . . . ἐν τούτῳ πιστεύομεν: He replies: ἄρτι πιστεύετε (xvi. 30 f). For $ν \hat{υ} ν$ = at the present time, ἄρτι = at this moment, see Abbott, *Voc.* 1719. Cf. ii. 10, xiii. 36 f.

[2] For this formula see iv. 23, v. 25, xii. 23, xvii. 1.

[3] σκορπισθῆτε is illustrated by x. 12 ὁ λύκος ἁρπάζει αὐτὰ καὶ σκορπίζει. For the fact see Mc. xiv. 50 (Mt. xxvi. 56).

[4] Cf. Jo. xix. 27 εἰς τὰ ἴδια.

The solitude of the Lord's human life must have been one of its deepest trials. He lived, it is true, in the company of twelve men, whom He had Himself chosen and appointed to be with Him; but in the inner life of His unique personality He was always alone. The Twelve could not share or understand His purposes, His motives, His burdens, or His rarer moments of rejoicing. True man, with the human craving for sympathy and fellowship, He lived His life at a level which no other human life ever attained; while the Twelve, as we see them portrayed in the Gospels, were not remarkable for either intellectual or spiritual gifts. But if His whole life was solitary beyond that of the most lonely of men, the climax of solitude was reached when sympathy was most sorely needed, in the Agony, the trials before the High Priests and the Roman procurator, the way to the Cross, and on the Cross itself. Alone the Lord left the garden, without a friend; alone He stood before Annas, Caiaphas, Pilate, Herod; alone, it seems, so far as ten of the Twelve were concerned, He lay dying on the Cross and gave up His spirit; the only human sympathy that was offered came from the unknown "daughters of Jerusalem" and the women that followed from Galilee.[1] But in the mystery of His Divine nature He was not alone, for the Father was with Him in

[1] Lc. xxiii. 27 ff., Mc. xv. 40 (Mt. xxvii. 55 f.).

unbroken fellowship. Only at one awful moment was the consciousness of that fellowship lost, and even then the withdrawal was relative only. The Lord's manhood cried, "Why hast thou forsaken me?" for it could not realize the Divine Presence. But the Presence remained; the sun was behind the cloud, and, before the end came, it shone out again.

So, with this note of true confidence in the Father's unfailing love, the Lord reaches the last words of His last discourse.

*These things I have spoken unto you that in me ye may have peace. In the world ye have distress; but take courage: I have conquered the world* (xvi. 33).

Another "I have spoken"[1] proclaims the actual completion of the Lord's teaching. The Last Discourse begins, "Let not your heart be troubled"; its first section ends, "My peace I give unto you," and the second, "That in me ye may have peace."[2] His peace, peace in Him and in God, is His remedy for heart-trouble. It is a peace not to be gained by flying from trouble, but by facing it: a peace which ensures not the absence of pain, but the certainty of conquest. Christ's peace did not guarantee for Him and does not guarantee for His disciples either physical or unmixed spiritual ease. While we are here we have

[1] λελάληκα : cf. xiv. 15, xv. 3, 11, xvi. 1, 4, 6, 25.
[2] xiv. 1, 27, xvi. 33.

always to do with another factor in life, even as He had: "In the world ye have tribulation." The peace of God, which Christ gives, does not protect from the troubles of life, but on the other hand it is not impaired by them. Peace and tribulation concur in the same experience, belonging to different spheres in our complex humanity. The world presses from without; Christ dwells within and gives His peace to the inward man.

Hence, in the face of imminent suffering and loss, Christ can bid the Eleven "take heart."[1] The call was familiar to them. They had heard Him speak so to the paralytic whose sins He forgave; to the woman who sought to steal a cure; to themselves when they saw Him walking, phantom-like, upon the sea, and cried out with fear.[2] And now, on this last night with Him before the Passion, in the last sentence of His last discourse, they heard it again. They knew that it meant the approach of danger, and was a call for a great effort on their part to exercise self-control, endurance, and strength of will; but they knew also that, if they made such an effort, it promised them peace and victory.

"Take heart," "be of good cheer." Why? The Lord does not add, as we might expect, "Ye shall overcome." Once more He draws their thoughts

[1] θαρσεῖτε.
[2] Mt. ix. 2, 22, Mc. vi. 50.

off from themselves, and fixes them on Him. "I have overcome the world"; you fight a vanquished enemy.

We are accustomed to think of Christ as the conqueror of sin and death. It is less usual to regard Him as the conqueror of the world. Yet such He was and knew Himself to be, even before the battle had been won. No other great leader of men ever ventured to speak thus on the eve of a battle which he foresaw would bring defeat and death. Jesus was about to conquer by death; to complete His victory over the world upon the Cross. "I have conquered," He says, as if the victory were already complete.[1] So, in effect, it was; to have lived without sin, to have been obedient to the point of death, to continue at His post in the face of the world's fierce enmity, was a victory to which it remained only to add to-morrow the last act of death. But why does He speak of His own victory rather than of theirs? Because His victory includes the victory of His Church, of all who by faith and hope make it their own. "They overcame," it is said of the martyrs, "because of the blood of the Lamb"; and of all believers, "This is the victory that overcometh the world, even our faith."[2] *Hoc vince*, 'Conquer by the

---

[1] Another perfect—$\nu\epsilon\kappa\iota\kappa\eta\kappa\alpha$. Looking back on His victory from the Throne He uses the aorist (Apoc. iii. 21).

[2] 1 Jo. v. 4 f., Apoc. xii. 11.

Cross,' goes further and deeper than Constantine knew; it is the motto that inspires every moral and spiritual victory.

So, with the battle yet raging or scarcely begun, the Church can "take heart," and say with St Paul when yet far from the end of his course, "In all these things we are more than conquerors through him that loved us."[1]

[1] Rom. viii. 37 ὑπερνικῶμεν διὰ τοῦ ἀγαπήσαντος ἡμᾶς.

*CUM ERGO DIXISSET PROPTER QUID OMNIA SIT LOCUTUS, UT IN ILLO SCILICET PACEM HABERENT... EO QUI ERAT AD ILLOS SERMONE FINITO, DEINDE AD PATREM VERBA DIREXIT, ET ORARE IAM COEPIT... PROINDE EAM QUAM FECIT ORATIONEM PRO NOBIS, NOTAM FECIT ET NOBIS; QUONIAM TANTI MAGISTRI NON SOLUM AD IPSOS SERMOCINATIO, SED ETIAM PRO IPSIS AD PATREM ORATIO, DISCIPULORUM EST AEDIFICATIO; ET SI ILLORUM QUI HAEC DICTA ADERANT AUDITURI, PROFECTO ET NOSTRA, QUI FUERAMUS CONSCRIPTA LECTURI.*

*AUGUSTINE.*

# THE LAST PRAYER

(ST JOHN XVII.)

πάντοτε ζῶν εἰς τὸ ἐντυγχάνειν ὑπὲρ αὐτῶν.

## I.

OF the prayers of Christ the Synoptic Gospels make frequent mention,[1] but give no detailed example, although they were sometimes offered aloud, as it appears, in the presence of the Twelve.[2] The prayer which St John gives at length after the Last Discourse arises out of the discourse, and in a manner continues it, turning Godward the principal thoughts and desires which the discourse had revealed to the Eleven. It stands, therefore, in direct relation to the preceding chapters, and completes their teaching, carrying it up to a higher plane, where it is seen in the light of the Divine Presence. The Teacher becomes the Intercessor; the Prophet, the High Priest. On the eve of Good Friday[3] He shews us what He will ask and receive from the Father when the Cross is past and He is at the Right Hand of God.[4]

---

[1] See Mc. i. 35, vi. 46, xiv. 35 ff.; Lc. v. 16, vi. 12, ix. 18, 28 f.

[2] See Lc. xi. 1.

[3] Jo. xvii. is appropriately read by the Church of England on Maundy Thursday.

[4] Cf. v. 1 ταῦτα ἐλάλησεν Ἰησοῦς, καὶ . . . εἶπεν.

*These things spake Jesus; and lifting up his eyes to heaven he said, Father, the hour is come; glorify thy Son that the Son may glorify thee* (xvii. 1).

The discourse ended, the prayer followed, as it seems, almost immediately.[1] One silent gesture, as the disciples noticed, marked the transition: He "lifted up His eyes to heaven."[2] The act pointed on the one hand to the creaturely nature[3] and earthly surroundings of the Son of Man; and, on the other, it spoke of the sinlessness which enabled Him to look up without fear into the Face of God.

"Father,"[4] the Lord begins, "the hour is come";[5] that is, the hour for the glorification of which He had spoken. The prayer takes up the note which He had struck at the outset. As Judas left the Supper-chamber He had said, "Now is the Son of Man glorified and God is glorified in Him."[6] The predestined hour has arrived at last, and He knows it; yet He prays for the fulfilment of that which was certain to come. There is no fatalism in the

[1] Aug. *tract.* cxv.: "poterat orare silentio, sed ita se Patri exhibere voluit precatorem, ut meminisset nostrum se esse doctorem."

[2] The gesture was probably in common use; cf. Lc. xviii. 13, where the τελώνης is singular in not adopting it: οὐκ ἤθελεν οὐδὲ τοὺς ὀφθαλμοὺς ἐπᾶραι εἰς τὸν οὐρανόν.

[3] For πάτερ (or πατήρ) without μου or ἡμῶν cf. Mc. xv. 34, Jo. xi. 41, xii. 27, xvii. 5, 11, 21, 24 f. So also in the Lord's prayer as given in the best text of Lc. xi. 2.

[4] Aug. *tract.* cxv.: "in forma servi et ex orma servi."

[5] Cf. vii. 30, viii. 20, xii. 23, 27, xiii. 1. [6] xiii. 31.

## ST JOHN XVII. 1, 2

Lord's foreknowledge; all is in the Father's hands, and He asks with filial submission and trust for its accomplishment. He asks for His own glorification through the Cross; for the glorification of the Incarnate Son is the glorification of the Father. A glorified Christ will not detract from the glory of God, but rather will manifest it to the world; that every knee should bow in the Name of Jesus, and every tongue confess Him to be the Lord, is to the glory of the Father who sent Him and whom He reveals.[1]

All this was in accordance with the Father's purpose in sending His Son into the world, and qualifying Him for His saving work. *According as thou gavest him authority over all flesh, that all that thou hast given him, he should give to them life eternal. But this is that eternal life, that they learn to know thee the only true God, and him whom thou didst send, Jesus Christ* (xvii. 2 f.).

The glorification of Jesus by the Cross and of the Father through the Son corresponds with the powers bestowed upon Him when He was sent to redeem the world. He had then received from the Father an authority which extends over all mankind, the mass of weak, mortal humanity.[2] The purpose of

---

[1] Phil. ii. 9-11.

[2] πᾶσα σάρξ = כָּל־בָּשָׂר: cf. Gen. vi. 12, Ps. lxxvii. 39, Isa. xl. 5; Mt. xiii. 20, 1 Pet. i. 24 (with Hort's note).

this Messianic authority,[1] this Headship of all humanity, was to enable the Son of Man to give eternal life to the whole body of believers which in His Divine foreknowledge the Father has given Him. But the eternal life which He is authorized to give consists in the knowledge of God and of His Christ: of God, the Only God who truly answers to that supreme Name[2]; of Jesus Christ,[3] as sent by the Only God, representing Him in the world, and exercizing His authority over mankind.

Our Lord is the "Author of life."[4] "That which hath been made—the whole creation—was life in Him"[5]; as the Eternal Word, He gave physical life to all that lives, and intellectual life to man. His mission into the world which He had made was also concerned with the giving of life, but of a life higher and fuller than that which He gave in creation. "I came," He says, "that they may have life, and have it in greater abundance."[6] Here He tells us in

---

[1] For the ἐξουσία of the Son of Man see Mc. ii. 10, Jo. v. 27, x. 18; and for the genitive of the subject over which the authority is exercised, Mc. vi. 7 ἐξ. τῶν πνευμάτων τῶν ἀκαθάρτων. A still larger claim is made in Mt. xxviii. 18. On the word ἐξουσία see Abbott, *Voc.* 1590 f.

[2] For [ὁ] μόνος θεός see Jo. v. 44, 1 Tim. i. 17, Jude 25, and for ὁ ἀληθινὸς θ. 1 Thess. i. 9, 1 Jo. v. 20.

[3] On the use of Ἰησοῦς Χριστός in this place see the notes of Westcott and Zahn.

[4] Acts iii. 15 τὸν δὲ ἀρχηγὸν τῆς ζωῆς ἀπεκτείνατε.

[5] Jo. i. 4 ὃ γέγονεν ἐν αὐτῷ ζωὴ ἦν (adopting WH's punctuation).

[6] x. 10.

what this better life consists. It is knowledge, the knowledge of God and of Christ; not a merely intellectual knowledge, but a spiritual intuition which implies conformity to the will of God, communion with Him, possession of Him. As truth in St John is the supreme Reality, so knowledge is spiritual apprehension of the highest Truth. Such knowledge is identical with the highest life, the life which lifts men up into the world of realities, and belongs to the eternal order of things.[1]

The knowledge which is life eternal has a double object, the Father and the Son: the only true God and His Christ. The Christian faith as taught by Christ, as taught in the creeds of the Catholic Church, is a true monotheism. We believe in One God, who is the Father, but whose unity does not exclude His only Son; in one Son, who is God, and of God. The only true God, the one God who truly answers to the conception of Godhead, is "not one only Person," but Father and Son in the unity of the Holy Ghost. He who does not know the Son does not truly know the only God; the knowledge which is eternal life embraces the knowledge of Christ.[2] Yet the knowledge which is life is more than the intellectual acceptance of a true faith. It converts the creed into a reality which our spirits can apprehend, and by which they live both here and beyond the

[1] See F. von Hügel, *Eternal Life*, p. 74 ff.   [2] Jo. v. 11 f.

grave.[1]  To give this life our Lord was sent, and He gives it to all who come to God by Him.

The Lord returns to His prayer for glorification. "*I glorified thee upon the earth, completing the work which thou hast given me to do. And now glorify thou me, Father, with thyself, with the glory which I had with thee before the world was*" (xvii. 4 f.).

'Thou didst send me, and I obeyed thy call throughout my human life. I glorified thee all my days on earth to this last evening, and thus I have completed my appointed work. Now I ask for the exaltation of the human nature which has thus become obedient even unto death. Receive it into Thine own immediate Presence; grant it to share the glory of Thy Throne. There, before the world was, when as yet there was no created thing, in the solitude of eternity, I was already with Thee;[2] there henceforth let my manhood reap the fruit of its obedience in a glory to which no creature has attained.'[3]

So far the Last Prayer has been a pouring out of the Incarnate Son's petitions for Himself. He has fulfilled His mission, and He now claims for His manhood the reward of His perfected work. Now He turns from Himself to His disciples, and the rest of the Prayer refers to the Eleven and those who followed them in the life of faith.

[1] Cf. 1 Cor. viii. 2 καθὼς δεῖ γνῶναι.
[2] Cf. Jo. i. 2 πρὸς τον θεόν, 18 εἰς τὸν κόλπον τοῦ πατρός.
[3] Compare the thought in Phil. ii. 9-12, Heb. xii. 2, Apoc. iii. 21.

## II.

*I manifested thy name to the men whom thou gavest me out of the world. They were thine, and thou gavest them to me, and they have kept thy word. Now they have learned that all things whatsoever thou gavest me are from thee; for the words which thou gavest me I have given them, and they for their part received them, and knew in truth that I came forth from thee, and believed that thou didst send me* (xvii. 6-8).

In the Discourse the Lord had claimed that the Twelve were His choice;[1] and so indeed they were, inasmuch as they had not first chosen Him, but He them. But looking at the matter from the Divine point of view, they were the Father's gift to Him; His choice had followed the Father's grant. They were the Father's by creation; they had been given to the Son to receive from Him the knowledge which is life eternal, and all who were present that last night had kept to the end the Divine message which they had heard from Him. Much of it had not been clearly

---

[1] xv. 16. Cf. Aug. *tract.* cvi.: "quos Deus Filius de mundo elegit cum Patre, idem ipse homo Filius de mundo accepit a Patre."

## THE LAST PRAYER

understood; much had fallen on deaf ears; much lay on the surface of inattentive minds, and would presently have been lost altogether, had not the Paraclete come to remind and to enlighten. Yet, on the whole, they had been faithful to their trust; and a great trust it was. To these men alone the Lord had manifested the Father's Name—had given the revelation which was to transform human life and to save the world.

What had been the result thus far? Now—at the end of their three years' training—they had firmly grasped one fundamental truth, the Divine origin of the teaching and mission of Jesus.[1] Of that all-important fact their faith would never lose its hold. A year ago Simon Peter, speaking for all, had said, "We have come to believe and know that Thou art the Holy One of God."[2] And that very night they had broken into the discourse with the cry, "We believe that thou camest forth from God."[3]

It was but a meagre response to all His care, and the Lord had expressed His dissatisfaction at the time. Yet their faith, such as it was, was sound, and their loyalty beyond suspicion; a solid foundation had been laid, on which the Universal Church might

---

[1] xvi. 29 ff.

[2] vi. 69 ἡμεῖς πεπιστεύκαμεν καὶ ἐγνώκαμεν ὅτι σὺ εἶ ὁ ἅγιος τοῦ θεοῦ.

[3] xvi. 30 πιστεύομεν ὅτι ἀπὸ θεοῦ ἐξῆλθες.

in due time be built. For the present there was no room for further teaching, and the Lord betakes Himself to prayer on their behalf.

*It is for them I ask ; it is not for the world I ask, but for those whom thou hast given me ; for they are thine, and all things that are mine are thine, and the things that are thine are mine, and I have been glorified in them* (xvii. 9 f.).

The scope of His present prayer is limited ; the Lord does not on this occasion intercede for the hostile world, though on the Cross He prayed for His crucifiers ; nor for the world as a whole, though He came to mediate on behalf of the human race ;[1] but only for those who are specially given to Him—for the Eleven who have been the companions of His ministry, and have kept the Father's word. To these on His last night Jesus devotes all His thoughts ; to these He had addressed His last discourse ; for these He offers His last prayer. They had a special lien upon His prayers, and on the Father's gracious acceptance. They were the Father's before they belonged to the Incarnate Son ; and now that they were Christ's, they were doubly the Father's, for all things[2] that belong to the Son belong to the Father also, even as those that belong to the Father are also the Son's. Moreover, they were not only the Son's, but they had brought glory to Him by being faithful to Him, and

[1] 1 Tim. ii. 3-5.     [2] τὰ ἐμά, τὰ σά : not οἱ ἐμοί, οἱ σοι.

continuing to be so to the very end.¹ And now the time had come when they had special need of His prayer and of the Father's protecting love:

*And I am no more in the world, and they are in the world, and I am coming to thee. Holy Father, keep them in thy name,* that name *which thou hast given me,*² *that they may be one as we are* (xvii. 11).

Jesus has already in thought and purpose left the world. All through these chapters, ever since Judas went, He thinks and speaks as one whose life is ended.² For He knows that to-morrow night will find Him in the tomb; He is already dead to the world of outward things. To Him the change will be gain, for it will bring Him on His way to the Father. But for the disciples who are left behind, the world without the Master will be not merely full of bitterness, but full of danger. They cannot follow Him now, and the Lord does not ask that they may. But there is safe keeping for them in the world, if His Father and theirs, the Source of holiness,³ spreads around them the protection of His Name, that revelation of His love and sanctity which He had given to His Son, and which the Son had already in part communicated to

---

[1] δεδόξασμαι ἐν αὐτοῖς.

[2] For ᾧ D² Vulg. read οὕς.

[3] Cf. xiii. 31, xiv. 25, xvi. 25 etc. With πάτερ ἅγιε cf. πατὴρ δίκαιε (v. 25). The epithet is not otiose in either case. God's holiness is the guarantee that He will keep His saints from the evil of the world; His justice forbids Him to abandon them.

## ST JOHN XVII. 11, 12

them. "The name of the Lord is a strong tower; the righteous runneth into it, and is safe."[1] If that was the experience of Old Testament saints, how much more would it be true of those who took refuge in the revelation of God which had been made by the Incarnate Son? One danger in particular the Lord feared for His disciples: the breaking up of the bonds of fellowship and brotherly love, the disruption and disintegration of the Christian society which He had founded in the world. Their safeguard lay in realizing the Fatherhood of God, as Jesus had revealed it; the unity of essence which joins inseparably the Father and the Son; the unity of holy love which binds together all believers in the Christian brotherhood.

*When I was with them I ever kept them in thy name which*[2] *thou hast given me, and I guarded them, and none of them perished but the son of perdition, that the Scripture might be fulfilled* (xvii. 12).

The Lord had not asked the Father to keep His disciples so long as He was with them; it was His own prerogative, as the Good Shepherd, to watch over His little flock, and He had done so day by day[3] through the progressive revelation of the Divine Name committed to Him. And in point of fact He had protected them so successfully that none was lost, except the one whose character had

---

[1] Prov. xviii. 10.  [2] For ᾧ AC³D Vulg. read οὕς.
[3] ἐτήρουν.

marked him out for that miserable end,[1] whose doom fulfilled the anticipations of Scripture.[2] No keeping, no protection, not even that of the Incarnate Son, could save the man who in the presence of Christ followed the trade of a thief.[3]

The rest of the Twelve had been kept and protected[4] hitherto; but that night would shew how dependent they were on the personal care of the Master. One of the Eleven would deny that he knew his Lord, and be saved from a fatal fall only by the prayers of Christ.[5] What would happen when He was taken from them, as He would presently be? Yet Jesus foresees for them not only safety but joy.

*But now I am coming to thee, and these things I speak*

---

[1] ὁ υἱὸς τῆς ἀπωλείας: cf. 2 Thess. ii. 3—not, as Augustine (*tract.* cvii.), "perditioni praedestinatus," but doomed by his own sinful habits. Similarly οἱ υἱοὶ τῆς βασιλείας (Mt. xiii. 38), τῆς ἀναστάσεως (Lc. xx. 36), τῆς ἀπειθίας (Eph. ii. 2). So τέκνα φύσει ὀργῆς (Eph. ii. 3), τοῦ φωτός (Eph. v. 3), τῆς ὑπακοῆς (1 Pet. i. 14). The Vulgate attempts to keep up the alliteration ἀπώλετο, ἀπωλείας (*perivit, perditionis*), and so the R.V. ("perished . . . perdition").

[2] The scripture referred to is probably Ps. xli. 9, already quoted in xiii. 18. Cf. Ps. cix. 8, quoted in Acts i. 20. There is no need to press the telic force of ἵνα here; the sense is nearly that of ὥστε ἡ γρ. ἐπληρώθη: a fuller meaning has been given to the Psalm by the sin and ruin of Judas.

[3] xii. 6.

[4] ἐτήρουν . . . ἐφύλαξα, Vulg. *observabam . . . custodivi*. The difference of tense corresponds to the difference of meaning: the keeping was constant, the guarding at moments of special danger, or, perhaps, the result of this keeping.

[5] Lc. xxii. 32.

*in the world, that they may have my joy fulfilled in themselves* (xvii. 13).

The Lord Himself was entering into the fulness of His joy, for to go to the Father was to Him joy unspeakable. It was His will not only to provide for the safe keeping of the disciples when He was gone, but to share with them His joy. He had spoken as He had in the Last Discourse, He was speaking as He did in His Last Prayer, that His words might inspire the Eleven with a hope which would in the end ripen into a joy such as His own. They would remember how He had promised them His abiding presence in the Spirit, how He had commended them to the keeping of the Father, and they would "rejoice in hope of the glory of God";[1] and the joy of hope would be one day fulfilled in the joy of fruition, the very joy of their Lord.[2]

[1] Rom. v. 2.      [2] Mt. xxv. 21, 23.

## III.

*I have given them thy word, and the world hated them because they are not of the world, as I am not of the world. I ask not that thou take them out of the world, but that thou keep them from the Evil One. Of the world they are not, as I am not of the world* (xvii. 14-16).

One great gift of God the Eleven had already received from Christ—His word, His revelation of Himself in the person and teaching of His Son. They had proof of it in the attitude of the world towards them; the possession of the word of God had impressed upon them a character which the world noted as alien and which it resented.[1] In the sight of the world it marked them, as it had marked the Master,[2] for citizens of another order whose standards and ideals were at variance with its own.

The world, then, hated Christ's disciples as it hated Christ. This would bring them suffering and loss.

[1] *ep. ad Diognetum* 6. 3 f. Χριστιανοὶ ἐν κόσμῳ οἰκοῦσιν, οὐκ εἰσὶ δὲ ἐκ τοῦ κόσμου . . . μισεῖ καὶ Χριστιανοὺς ὁ κόσμος μηδὲν ἀδικούμενος.

[2] Aug. *tract.* cviii.: "illi iam non de mundo quia renati . . . ille nunquam de mundo quia natus est de Spiritu sancto."

Yet Christ does not ask for them any shortening of their life on earth, any premature removal from the present order to another and a better.

Of the world His true disciples can never be, even as He Himself never was of it. To be of the world is one thing, to be in it another; the first is impossible for Christ and for those that are His, the second is not only possible but necessary and expedient. It was necessary for Him to be in the world that He might fulfil His mission, offer His sacrifice, found His Church. To be in the world is necessary also for His disciples, for it is through conflict with the world that their victory is won, and through their work in the world that the world itself is to be saved. Christ, therefore, does not ask for their removal from the world till the victory has been gained and the work done. He asks only for safe keeping, and for this only in regard to the forces of evil which are in the world and by which it is ruled. As He bids His disciples pray "Deliver us from evil," so when He prays for them He asks that they may be kept from evil. In neither prayer is there any petition for deliverance from suffering; in both it is moral evil which is deprecated. In both, again, moral evil assumes, as it seems, a personal form.[1] It is

[1] Both in the Lord's prayer and in the present context the gender is uncertain (ἀπὸ τοῦ πονηροῦ, ἐκ τοῦ πονηροῦ). But ὁ πονηρός is beyond dispute in Mt. xiii. 19, and in 1 Jo. ii. 13 f., v. 18; and the masculine accords with our Lord's usual insistence on the personality of evil.

## THE LAST PRAYER

the personal force which lies behind sin that the Lord, with His profound sense of the inner meaning of life, dreads for its assaults upon His disciples. The Ruler of the world had nothing in Him,[1] but has much in each of His followers, and knows how to use to the best advantage the foothold which Christians suffer him to gain.

The Lord continues to pray for His disciples: *Consecrate them in the truth: thy word is truth. As thou didst send me into the world, so I also sent them into the world; and on their behalf I consecrate myself, that they also may be consecrated to truth* (xvii. 17-19).

More is needed by the disciples of Christ than safe keeping from evil. They require also a lifelong consecration to God; "Consecrate them," the Lord prays: "I consecrate myself that they also may be consecrated." The word is constantly used in the Greek Old Testament for the dedication of men and things to the service of God.[2] Here it is used to express the consecration of spirit which comes from the truth,[3] *i.e.* from the revelation of God in Christ; "thy word," the Lord adds, "is truth." The truth consecrates, by claiming for God the intellectual and spiritual nature of man, of which

---

[1] xiv. 30.

[2] For $ἁγιάζειν$ in the sense of consecrating persons or things to the service of God, see Exod. xiii. 2, xxix. 21, xl. 9, Lev. xvi. 4, Deut. xv. 19, 2 Sam. viii. 11, etc (LXX).

[3] $ἐν\ τῇ\ ἀληθείᾳ$ (cf. $ἐν\ ἀληθείᾳ$, *v.* 19).

it takes possession; the mind and heart which the truth makes its own are dedicated to the "Holy Father," and can no longer be given to the world, even as a consecrated building or instrument cannot without sacrilege be turned to secular uses.

The Lord speaks again of that which He Himself had experienced. The Father had consecrated Him[1] and sent Him into the world. In His case consecration can only mean the Father's eternal predestination of the Person of the Son for the special service of the Incarnation, and the Son's willing acceptance of that great mission. As the Father had consecrated and sent the Son, so now the Son sends the Eleven into the world and prays the Father to consecrate them by the word of truth which He has revealed through the mission of the Son. Between the consecration of the Lord and the consecration of the disciples there is an intimate connexion. The Lord was at that very moment responding to the Father's predestination which called Him to the Cross, and thus consecrating Himself[2] in time as He had been consecrated by the Father in His preexistent life. In the words "I consecrate myself," He admits us to the sanctuary of His human will, where He is now preparing Himself for the supreme act of obedience. He does this, no doubt, in fulfilment of the Father's will, but He does it also for the

[1] Jo. x. 36 ὃν ὁ πατὴρ ἡγίασεν.   [2] ἁγιάζω ἐμαυτόν (v. 19).

sake of His disciples,[1] to make possible their consecration through His own. Only through His great self-surrender can they be consecrated indeed. His sacrifice will open the way for their approach to God, His example will inspire them with devotion; and so they will in their measure be consecrated [2] as the Lord was consecrated, and can be sent into the world, as He was sent, to fulfil God's purpose in the salvation of men.

[1] ὑπὲρ αὐτῶν.

[2] Cf. 1 Cor. i. 2 ἡγιασμένοις ἐν Χριστῷ Ἰησου, vi. 11 ἡγιάσθητε, Heb. x. 10, 29 τὸ αἷμα . . . ἐν ᾧ ἡγιάσθη, xiii. 12; elsewhere the writer to the Hebrews seems to prefer the idea of a continuous consecration (ii. 11 οἱ ἁγιαζόμενοι, x. 14).

## IV.

The Master proceeds with His prayer. *Yet not for these only do I ask, but also for those who believe*[1] *on me through their word* (xvii. 20).

The Last Prayer is not for the world; so the Lord has already said. But on the other hand it is not limited to the narrow circle of the Apostles. Jesus looks beyond the ranks of His first disciples, and sees an ever-growing company of believers; now indifferent or hostile, but soon to be brought to the faith by the teaching of those whom He Himself had taught: the three thousand to be added on the day of Pentecost, the "many myriads" of Jews who believed[2] some thirty years later; the churches that before the first generation had died out began to shine as lights in the world, throughout the Empire and beyond it. Nor need we restrict His foresight to these; it stretches surely far beyond the first century and reaches to ourselves. All generations of the Church have received their knowledge of Christ ultimately from the "word" of these eleven

[1] πιστευόντων ℵABCD*, πιστευσόντων D² Vulg.
[2] Acts xxi. 20.

men[1] which has come down to us in the traditional faith of Christendom as well as in the written documents of the first age. How far all this was present in detail to the human mind of the Lord we cannot tell, but it justifies us in claiming for ourselves and for those who will follow a place in the Lord's last prayer.

What does He ask for this great company? *That they may all be one, as thou, Father, art in me and I am in thee—that they also may be in us,*[2] *that the world may believe that thou didst send me* (xvii. 21).

The Lord's prayer for the Eleven had been that they might be one as the Father and the Son are one. And now He extends this prayer to the whole Church in all time, "that they may all be one" with a unity corresponding to the unity of the Father and the Son. The Divine unity consists, as we know, in identity of nature and a perfect fellowship of spirit, together with a constant interchange of the Divine life in such wise that the Father is ever in the Son and the Son ever in the Father. This unity can be but imperfectly realized in created beings such as we are, each of whom is a separate centre of consciousness and self-determination; but it may reflect itself in oneness of faith and hope and love, in the com-

---

[1] Aug. *tract.* cix.: "quotquot enim postea crediderunt in eum, per verbum apostolorum sine dubio crediderunt." St Paul is hardly an exception, as regards the facts; cf. 1 Cor. xv. 3 ὃ καὶ παρέλαβον.

[2] ἵνα καὶ αὐτοὶ ἐν ἡμῖν ὦσιν. Before ὦσιν ℵAC³L insert ἕν, probably from *v.* 22.

munion of saints, and the fellowship of a common spiritual life. St Paul expresses this unity of spirit in the surprising phrase, "Ye are all one [man] in Christ Jesus."[1] The Church with its many members is "one man"; as the Persons in the Godhead are One God. The analogy is imperfect, but it is real, so far as our imperfect nature can answer to the Divine perfection. Moreover, the Lord desires that this unity of believers may be based on their union with God in Christ: "that they also may be in us." "Our communion," St John says elsewhere, "is with the Father and with His Son Jesus Christ";[2] and those who have fellowship with the Father and the Son cannot but have fellowship with one another in God.

The union of believers with one another in the Father and the Son is in its essence spiritual and not visible or external. Yet it ought to result in a visible union, which will appeal to the world that has no eye for the purely spiritual. The Lord has always in view the conversion of the world, and in the visible co-operation of all His followers He sees the most important of instruments for bringing about that great event. The world, He has taught, is to be convicted and convinced by the Paraclete, but when this has been done, it will still be a

[1] Gal. iii. 28 πάντες γὰρ ὑμεῖς εἷς ἐστὲ ἐν Χριστῷ Ἰησοῦ.
[2] 1 Jo. i. 3.

long way off from faith. The spectacle of brotherly love which it witnessed in the early days of the Church[1] might have brought it to faith, had not the brightness of the vision been clouded over by the growing divisions of Christendom. Our own age at last shews signs of an approach if not to the reunion of the churches, yet to the settlement of the preliminaries of peace; and there are practical steps which may now be taken on all sides without compromise of principle. By taking these our generation may set forward not only the cause of unity, but a cause even more vital and dearer to the heart of Christ, that of winning the world to the obedience of faith.

*And I have given them the glory which thou hast given me, that they may be one as we are one, I in them, and thou in me, that they may be perfected into one; that the world may come to know that thou didst send me, and lovedst them as thou lovedst me* (xvii. 22 f.).

The unity of all believers, which reflects the unity of the Father and the Son, depends upon a gift which the Lord has already given to His Church. He has given her for this purpose the glory[2] which He has Himself received from the Father. "We beheld His glory," the Evangelist has said in the

---

[1] See xiii. 34 ff., xv. 17.
[2] On δόξα see Abbott, *Son of Man*, 3571 ff.

prologue to his Gospel, " glory as of an only-begotten from a father." The Father gave it to the Only-begotten Son in the mystery of the eternal generation. He had this glory before the world was, when He dwelt, God with God,[1] in the yet unrevealed sanctuary of the Divine Life. And this glory, so far as it can be imparted, He has given to all who believe in Him; not indeed His unique Sonship, not His incommunicable Godhead, but the glory of the Divine character; the Love which unites the Father and the Son, and is the Spirit of Both.[2] This the Son can and does impart, and it is this which gives to the Church a unity analogous to that which exists in the interior life of God. By virtue of this Gift the Incarnate Son is in all believers as the Father is in the Son, and thus they are brought, so far as their limited nature permits, into a perfect unity to which nothing is wanting, and of which there will be no end. Through the Spirit the members of the Church are one with the Father and the Son, and their union with God in Christ brings with it union with one another in the One Body of Christ. When this union has again become visible through the restoration of an external fellowship, the world itself will recognize the supernatural beauty of the Church's common

---

[1] i. 1 ἦν πρὸς τὸν θεόν, καὶ θεὸς ἦν.

[2] See Augustine, *de trin.* xv. 31 ff.; cf. *The Holy Spirit in the Ancient Church*, p. 331 ff.

life, and gather from it the Divine mission of Jesus Christ, and that the Divine Love rests upon the members of Christ as it rested on Himself. So the dim sense which the world has always had that the Church belongs to another order, and has relations with an unseen and eternal world, will grow with the growing manifestation of her God-like unity, until it comes to know what it has long suspected, and to confess that God is in us of a truth.

## V.

*Father, that which thou hast given me, I will that where I am they also be with me, that they may behold my glory which thou hast given me, for thou lovedst me before the foundation of the world*[1] (xvii. 24).

The Lord recalls the two great gifts which He received in the past eternity from the Father. The Father not only gave Him, in the act of generation, His own Godhead and glory, but gave Him also, in His eternal purpose, all who should in time believe on His Name. He thinks of all these as a single gift—"that which thou hast given me";[2] and it is His desire that they may be at last gathered from all the generations of mankind into a single company in the glory of His presence. At the beginning of the Last Discourse He had promised the Eleven, "I will receive you to myself, that where I am ye may be also."[3] Now He claims from the Father the fulfilment of this promise, not to the Eleven only,

---

[1] With πρὸ καταβολῆς κόσμου, cf. Eph. i. 41; Pet. i. 20 (with Hort's note).

[2] Cf. xvii. 2 πᾶν ὃ δέδωκας αὐτῷ δώσει αὐτοῖς ζωὴν αἰώνιον.

[3] xiv. 3.

but to all who are His by the Father's gift. "Father, I will": He no longer asks, but wills. Later that night, in the garden, He is careful to say, "Not what I will, but what thou wilt."[1] Here there is no such reservation, for He knows that the Father wills what He wills; it is the Father's will, as it is His, that those who have been given to Him shall be with Him; for that end they were given. And He adds the reason why He wills to have them with Him: that with the eyes of the spiritual body they may behold His glory, as they could not behold it here and now. He uses the word 'behold'[2] and not 'see,' for it is not of the vision of mere faith that He speaks here, but of the revelation to be made hereafter to the whole nature of man: the revelation of the Incarnate Word in His glorified humanity. When our human nature has been raised and transferred, as His has been, into the spiritual and eternal order, there will be, He seems to teach, a renewal of the visualized presence of the Lord, to be apprehended by faculties of which in our present state we have no experience. "We shall see Him as He is,"[3] and discern in Him the glory which He had with the Father before creation began; that eternal gift of the Father's love

---

[1] Mc. xiv. 36.

[2] $\theta\epsilon\omega\rho\hat{\omega}\sigma\iota\nu$, not $\dot{o}\rho\hat{\omega}\sigma\iota\nu$. Contrast xvi. 16 οὐκέτι θεωρεῖτέ με . . . ὄψεσθε.

[3] 1 Jo. iii. 2.

of which we ourselves have received a measure in the gift of the Spirit of Christ. If this is His will, who can doubt that it will be accomplished, though as yet we know not how?

*Righteous Father, the world*[1] *knew thee not, but I knew thee, and these knew that thou didst send me. And I made known to them thy name, and will make it known, that the love with which thou lovedst may be in them, and I in them* (xvii. 25 f.).

These last words of the Prayer sum up all. They reveal God as "Father," the God of infinite love, yet "righteous,"[2] a Father whose love is tempered and conditioned by absolute justice and truth. The mission of His Son into the world has shewn that though the world professed to know God, in fact it knew Him not, since it did not recognize His only Son and very Image. There was but one exception, Jesus Himself, who as the Son of Man knew God, living in constant sinless communion with Him. The Eleven had not known God as their Master knew Him, but they had made the great and vital discovery that

---

[1] καὶ ὁ κόσμος ... ἐγὼ δέ ... καὶ οὗτοι, the world on the one hand—I and these on the other: cf. Abbott, *Gr.* 2164: "the first καὶ is intended to keep the reader in suspense ... the sentence is broken by a parenthesis."

[2] Cf. πάτερ ἅγιε (*v.* 11). For δίκαιος in this connexion see Rom. iii. 26, 1 Jo. i. 9, Apoc. xvi. 5. While ἅγιος represents God in the unique majesty of His separation from the finite and sinful, δίκαιος on the other hand emphasizes His relations with the creature and, in particular, with man.

Jesus came from God and had a Divine message for the world. Even this limited knowledge of the Son had lifted them above the world, and prepared them to know the Father who sent Him.

To this little flock of loyal hearts the Son made known [1] the Father's Name as they were able to bear it. And His teaching was not yet at an end; He would continue to teach by His Spirit.[2] The revelation of the Father would go forward after the coming of the Spirit with a new plainness of speech, contrasting sharply with the mystery and reserve of the Lord's earthly teaching.[3] As the Spirit continued to reveal the Divine Fatherhood, the Divine righteousness, there would arise in the souls of the faithful a deepening consciousness of the Divine love abiding in them, the same love that rested on the Only-begotten Son;[4] and with it the sense of Christ's presence, dwelling in the heart by faith. "I in them,"[5] with the implied counterpart, "they in me," completes the circle of the gifts and blessings which the Lord desires for His members upon earth.

So the prayers of Jesus Christ, the Incarnate Son of God, are ended.[6] They have reached the furthest limit of human desire and hope. The Son Himself

---

[1] Cf. xv. 15.     [2] γνωρίσω.     [3] Cf. xvi. 12. 25 ff.

[4] Aug. *tract.* cx.: "qui enim diligit Unigenitum profecto diligit et membra eius."

[5] Not σὺ ἐν αὐτοῖς, though that is in some sense also true; see xiv. 23.

[6] Cf. Ps. lxxii. 20.

can ask no more for those whom the Father has given Him, while they are here; the love of God and the presence of Christ in the communion of the Holy Spirit is all that in their present life they need or can receive. The Lord can now go forth to die; the work of His life on earth is done.

www.ingramcontent.com/pod-product-compliance
Lightning Source LLC
Chambersburg PA
CBHW051053160426
43193CB00010B/1169